THE
DIGITAL
CHARITY

Becoming a digital leader
in the non-profit sector

Matt Saunders

Michael Terence
Publishing

First published in paperback by
Michael Terence Publishing in 2020
www.mtp.agency

ISBN 9781913289881

Cover by Will Saunders

Contents

FOREWORD

It is now more than a quarter of a century since the first charity websites were built. Since then "online" has become "digital", and the term "World Wide Web" acquired a quaintly archaic tone. A whole generation has started working in the charity sector who have grown up knowing only a digital world, to the extent that "digital" itself is an almost superfluous term.

Yet this is the ideal time for a book that guides you through making the most of your charity's digital presence. In particular, it is the right time for a book that works from first principles and assumes that you don't necessarily have to hand the combined experience of the past 25 years of digital activity in the charity sector.

It is essential because the digital canvas has grown rapidly, with an endless choice of tools and approaches. And these appear to be expanding at an ever-increasing and challenging rate.

Matt Saunders has distilled much of his commercial and charity digital experience, and that of others, into a practical guide book that mercifully lets you take a step back and take a breath.

He rightly focuses on building and enhancing a website to serve as the hub that supports all that the charity strives for. Social media, email, CRMs, analytics, personas, and third-party integrations are all covered, but rooted to the power of an effective website.

The book is written for those with varying degrees of digital expertise, and simply assumes that its readers want to harness the evident power of a website to support their charity.

Its clear structure enables anyone to dip in at the stage they've reached. Beginners can work their way through the questions of why and how to build a website, and how much it might cost. More experienced users can dip in further on to learn more about search engine optimisation, generating revenue, and ensuring accessibility.

The title "The Digital Charity" says it all - digital isn't about the technology: it's about the charity and how to maximise its life-changing impact through communication, services and connecting people.

Howard Lake, UK Fundraising

INTRODUCTION

There are nearly 2 billion websites on the internet. Most of them are terribly ineffective at doing what they set out to do, whether that is to generate leads or sales, or simply to build brand awareness. In the third sector, the main role of the charity website is to grow awareness, generate a sustainable stream of income, and build a base of long-term supporters.

But all too often, website projects get rushed, or drag on until stagnant, leaving stakeholders disinterested and disheartened. *The Digital Charity* teaches you how to effectively navigate the website development process, inspiring your team to create an asset that finally works for your organisation.

How do you scope and deliver a great website for your charity? How do you measure project success? How do you maintain momentum to ensure your website works hard for your organisation after launch? These are just some of the questions I'll be exploring using my 15 years of experience in the digital sector.

Your website is at the heart of your whole marketing strategy. It is the hub at the centre of your marketing wheel. With the advice and tips in this book, learn how to create the best, most effective website for your charity, gain confidence and become a digital leader in the sector.

Who is this book for?

This book is for charities. Specifically, it is for people who work in, volunteer for or govern charities. Even more specifically, it is for time-poor or money-poor organisations who know they *can* have a greater impact using digital technology, but are not sure *how*.

Perhaps you're a fundraiser who wants to build an additional income stream via your website. Or maybe you work in comms and need a platform that finally serves your marketing needs. Maybe you are a trustee who wants to demonstrate true digital leadership to your team.

In any case, if you're passionate about your work and your impact, and want to build a modern, sustainable online presence; this book is for you.

What will you learn?

This book takes a holistic look at the process of developing, launching and marketing a successful website for your charity. A website development project does not need to be expensive, or even lengthy, but it does require commitment. This book will help you to understand the core principles behind a successful website project, from assembling a team and preparing a brief, to pre-empting and resolving conflict, devising a marketing strategy, and measuring success.

The ultimate goal of this book is to empower you to make confident, informed decisions to develop the best digital experience for your supporters, service users and staff. This will naturally result in the creation of an incredibly valuable asset for your charity that goes on performing long after launch.

In Chapter 1 I explore some open questions you can ask to start building the case for a new website. I tackle the thorny issue of cost, and outline some methods you can use to get senior buy-in. Chapter 2 helps you to understand whether your organisation needs a visual refresh, and Chapter 3 gives you the tools you'll need to plan the shape of your project. In Chapter 4 I talk about content management, helping you to decide the platform upon which to build your website, and offer some industry tips on what questions to ask a professional website developer. In Chapter 5 I cover the importance of producing engaging content and give you some tips on how to achieve this, and in Chapter 6 I help you to strengthen your presence in search engines like Google. Chapter 7 looks at how you can get involved in online communities to spread the word about your work, and in Chapter 8 I explain how persona design can help to make sure you talk to the right people. In Chapter 9 I explain how to create an inclusive online service, and give real-world examples to this effect. In Chapters 10 and 11 I help you to understand how you can tap into a rich ecosystem of third-party tools via API integrations, and describe how to plug a CRM database into your website to foster stakeholder relationships. Chapter 12 provides guidance and support when it comes to managing your team, and Chapters 13 and 14 articulate how you can generate sustainable revenue and measure your marketing effectively. In Chapter 15, I share with you some valuable insights gained from interviewing charity professionals when writing this book, and Chapters 16 and 17 are designed to help you put your learning into practice.

For reference, you'll also find a helpful and comprehensive list of some common industry words and phrases in the Glossary of Key Terms. I explain these in clear English so that you can confidently communicate with your team and your suppliers to truly take advantage of all that the digital world offers.

How to use this book

The central goal of this book is to empower you to develop a successful website for your organisation, and I have written it in such a way that the broad direction of travel is A to B. That being said, there are a number of important aspects concerning the digital ecosystem that should be considered if your website project is to be a success. Topics such as search engine optimisation, stakeholder relationship management and social media marketing are all areas that would benefit from being covered during your website project, but equally they could be visited at a later date. Think of the path this book takes as a highway that branches off at points to cover related and important topics. Meander down these side streets, if you choose, or sail past and make a note to return to them later.

Who am I and why should you listen to me?

Hi, I'm Matt. For over 15 years I've worked in the digital sector. Here I will share with you some of my professional credentials, but if you'd like to hear my story and learn why I do what I do, refer to My Story.

During my time in the sector I have worked on so many projects, it would be impossible to recall every one of them. Some notable occurrences include the time I was given the opportunity to work on Stephen Fry's personal homepage, build a website to promote a book written by a former soap star and work with somebody who went on to pitch for investment on Dragons' Den. Oh, and there was that time I was asked to run code upgrades on British rapper Dizzy Rascal's website. It's funny the opportunities that come your way when you start getting your name out there.

For the past few years my focus has been on helping charities deliver digital projects. My first project in the non-profit sector was to deliver a secure online forum for those affected by CSE (Child Sexual Exploitation). This was part of a pilot programme and, after being hailed a success, still runs today (see Chapter 15 for a case study on this project). Shortly after, I was commissioned by another charity to help build an online platform for their beneficiaries, this time school students who would set up companies to help develop their confidence and entrepreneurial skills. Hearing about how the programme would turn previously-shy students into confident young professionals in the making cemented my desire to work more in the charity sector. Since then I've worked with charities large and small to provide digital consultancy, build online income streams, improve service user experience and deliver staff training.

I've scaled the walls of the digital industry (and bashed my head on a few) in project management roles, marketing positions and of course, website design. Working across disciplines has given me a unique insight into how digital projects operate, from their inception to completion. I get how it all "hangs together". I've seen how successful projects integrate the function of marketing, design and management, and how the diverse personalities of delivery teams can make or break an idea.

By drawing on the wealth of my experience working with a vast number of organisations and in various capacities, I distil down the key ingredients needed to plan, develop and deliver effective digital projects for non-profit organisations. *The Digital Charity* shares the culmination of my knowledge and experience to date, and I can't wait to see what you do with it.

Keeping in touch

If you find this book helpful, I'd love to hear from you! I'd also welcome any questions or comments you have on the content shared here. You can connect with me online in the usual places:

Twitter: twitter.com/WeAreCharityBox

LinkedIn: linkedin.com/in/mattsaunders

YouTube: bit.ly/2SSiup5

Email: matt.saunders@charitybox.io

To watch the video interviews I conducted when writing this book, visit thedigitalcharity.co.uk and to learn more about my work, visit charitybox.io.

Chapter 1:
BUILDING THE CASE

If you're reading this book, you are probably quite well sold on the idea that a good website is a sound and necessary investment for your organisation. I commend you for this; there are plenty in the sector who unfortunately don't see things in quite the same way. A report[1] commissioned by Lloyds Bank in 2018 revealed that 18% of UK charities had "no interest" in going online, and a staggering 31% saw being online as "not relevant".

Expect resistance.

Some people are afraid of the unknown, afraid to spend money and are wary of technology in general. These concerns are not entirely without merit, with instances of online fraud, data breaches and changes in privacy law making headlines regularly. This, coupled with a great, big question mark over the true value of "digital" in general, makes it easy to see why some people are turned off by the idea and want to stick with what they know.

But you and I know differently. The way we communicate is ever-changing. Young and old alike now use the web to access services, discuss ideas, buy

---

[1] https://resources.lloydsbank.com/pdf/bdi-report-2018.pdf

products and get information. The charities who thrive within this communication revolution are the ones who embrace change.

Did you know?

The way that we communicate is changing. When Shelter Scotland enlisted the help of a chatbot to field enquiries about changing renting legislation in 2017, they discovered that many people were "confident using a chatbot" on the website, and tracked over 6,500 interactions with the bot over a three month trial period.[2]

Starting the conversation

You know that an effective website is your passport to sustainability and growth. A well-planned website can develop extra funding streams for your charity, as well as save you time by acting as an information portal for stakeholders. When engaging in discussions around the provision of a new website, you can start by exploring a few open questions:

---

[2] https://blog.scotland.shelter.org.uk/can-a-chatbot-help-your-charity/

Why get a new website?

In my experience the answer to this question is generally "because our current one does nothing for us". Sometimes, a poor website can actively harm the organisation by appearing unprofessional. But let's scratch the surface a little more; is it not generating any donations? Is it too time-intensive to maintain? Is it simply past its use-by date? Knowing why you need a new website, and what function it will perform, is central to building your case. To get a handle on this, it's a good idea to look at how others in your space are operating. What competitive advantages do other organisations have? What are they doing that you are not? Whether competitors or collaborators, exploring the landscape around you can help you to understand where you fit in the picture.

What is currently wrong?

This is linked to the previous question, and can help to articulate in more detail how your current website might actually be damaging your charity. Think about it: your website has the potential to draw in new supporters, engage your fundraisers and increase your overall income. Imagine the cost in *lost gains*, and quantify it to use when building your case. If you can confidently claim that a new website will contribute toward an additional £25k a year in terms of donations, increase your brand exposure and help build partnerships, it becomes hard to argue against.

Additionally, you might reach out to colleagues and service users to uncover their pain points. Perhaps your current website is really hard to manage and staff struggle with it, or maybe it is unclear how beneficiaries can engage in your service because some vital content is missing on your current website. Finally, take a look at your current website's analytics, if you have this facility. If your engagement metrics tell a bleak story, use this data to help build your case. See Chapter 14 on how to understand your web analytics.

What are the associated timescales and fees?

Decision-makers will always query their investments on time and money. "How long is a piece of string?" is a common reply, but this book will help you to articulate your requirements and vision more clearly. This will enable you to understand how much budget you might allocate for the project. Knowing your budget is critical, as it will help professional service providers, such as website developers, to provide a more accurate quote. Having a reasonably accurate idea of the investment needed will also help bolster your case for a new website.

How much does a website actually cost?

We are naturally inclined to question the cost of something, but this question can be a red herring. There are a plethora of providers in the website development space, from pay monthly subscription models, off-shore development teams, established creative agencies and independent freelancers. Because of this, the costs vary enormously. Company X might quote you £2,000 where Company Y estimates anywhere up to £20,000 for largely the same product. The question is not really one of cost, but of value received. In the web design industry we sometimes talk of "brochureware" websites vs "dynamic" websites. Though this terminology is now a little dated, it can still be used to indicate your overall requirements. A website with only several pages, a blog and a third-party donation feature such as JustGiving would probably be considered "brochureware" because it is relatively simple from a technical perspective. However, a website with an online store, a membership system and an integrated donation feature would certainly require a heftier investment. It is worth also considering the service element of your project: are you looking for a functional developer who will simply get the job done, or do you need a more guided and personal service?

Another way to look at the question of budget is to interrogate your sense of value to understand what is most important to you. There is an established model for doing this, called the *project management triangle*. For the purpose of applying its principles to a website design project, let's take a look at three criteria: Good, Fast and Cheap.

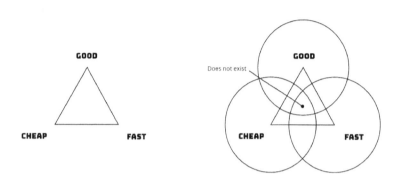

Everybody wants their project to be high quality, low cost and quickly delivered. But the reality is that this combination does not exist. Therefore, you must pick two priorities:

Good + Fast = Higher priced

Cheap + Fast = Lower quality

Good + Cheap = Slower to produce

This model is obviously a little rough and ready, but can be used to help you express your priorities and find out where you might need to compromise. Is quality important right now, or can you improve things later on? Are there budgetary restraints or can you make a significant investment? Have an honest and open conversation with your team about which aspects mean the most to you, and don't be coy about it with your chosen provider. Most suppliers are looking for a partnership, and will work with you to deliver the best solution they can with the resources you have.

What makes an effective website?

I use the word "effective" here for a reason: your website is a business tool that needs to deliver on your goals, whatever they may be. There is much talk of *innovation* and *creativity* in the design sector, but in most cases a website doesn't need to push any boundaries - it simply needs to work. Of course, that is not to say that something cannot be both beautiful and practical; Apple dressed their entire brand around it, but it is very important to understand that this is not an exercise in cosmetics. Core to the process of developing an *effective* website is understanding the goals of your organisation as well as being able to clearly articulate what your users want to get out of it. An effective website answers a visitor's question in seconds. An effective website loads quickly and works on whatever device the visitor is using. A visually-striking design can assist with engagement, but the priority is to support the user's goal in the quickest and simplest way possible. My advice is to focus your imagination on how to best give people what they want, rather than aesthetics, as without that foundation your project risks offering style over substance.

Getting buy-in

When you spend some time researching what is achievable using digital tools and how it can revolutionise your organisation, investing in this area becomes a no-brainer. The challenge now is to pull together your findings into a business case that compels your management or trustees to move forward with your ideas.

Step 1: Speak their language

The model for receiving funding often relies on having a documented "theory of change". In case you're not familiar with this, the theory of change is the process by which non-profits can predict and measure their impact. For example, let's imagine your charity exists to combat loneliness in older people. Your funding bid would outline how you will use the money to achieve your goal. You might state that you will run a number of events: social meetups, digital inclusion classes and so on, as well as gather evidence through questionnaires and conversations to understand how your events are being received by service users. You would track service user feedback over time, as well as the number of attendees (including returning attendees) and you would put forecasts in place in your funding bid to state your predicted outcomes. This is a *theory of change* or, if I were being a little more hard-nosed about it, the funder's return on investment (ROI).

Be sure to speak the language of the funder when putting the business case forward. How can your website and wider digital presence support *your* theory of change?

Step 2: Make it simple to understand

It's likely that your business case will be quite lengthy but remember: nobody wants to read long, dry documents. Don't omit the necessary detail, but consider extracting important or interesting points in order to make the benefits clear to see.

Step 3: Use evidence

In step 1 we explored the theory of change and how you can use this to make predictions of output based on input. That's useful, but it also helps to leverage evidence when building your case. Can you find any case studies by others in your sector who have achieved what you're hoping to achieve? Is there research available that will support your ideas? Seek out hard numbers and direct quotes from those involved in similar projects, and add these to your case.

Step 4: Paint a picture

If my time in marketing has taught me one thing it is that ideas must inspire. In my experience, bad ideas expressed well often trump good ideas expressed poorly, unfortunately. Be *aspirational,* and paint a picture of what could be achieved if you invest in the future.

Step 5: Use fear

Hopefully, you won't need this step, but it's handy to keep up your sleeve. If your project doesn't happen, what might be the consequences of this? A tapering off of support over time? A drop in volunteers, who see your organisation as archaic? Fear-based persuasion tactics can be a little iffy, in my opinion, but when used appropriately they can be effective.

It's an investment, not a cost

Above all else, the key message when seeking sign-off on any new project is to frame it as an investment. You are putting money into something in order to yield a greater return. This chapter has given you the ammunition you need to challenge the common perception that marketing activities are simply a cost, and the tools you need to confidently make your case.

Next up, we'll be looking at the topic of visual identity, and helping you decide if now is the right time for a rebrand.

Chapter 2:
DECIDING WHETHER TO REBRAND

Often, there is a catalyst for building a new website. A new CEO perhaps, with fresh ideas, or maybe it's the urgent need to appear more professional in order to win some vital funding. In any case, a website development project can present a great opportunity to conduct a wider review of your organisation's "front of house", and this includes your visual identity.

Before I go any further let me define what I mean by "visual identity" for those who may not be familiar with the term. The word "brand" refers to the way that people experience your organisation on a sensory level. It envelopes everything from vision and sound, to touch, taste and scent. In the same way you might identify a clothing brand by its style, or assess its price by the feel of the material, you know you're approaching a Subway when the familiar smell of their baking bread drifts down the street. This is brand identity in action.

"Visual identity" is, perhaps unsurprisingly, the visual aspect of brand, and it is usually what we're referring to when we are talking about "brand". In this context, brand refers to the look and feel of your organisation, from its logo and colours, to its typographic styles and the mood it creates using photography or illustration. You'll note how charities who have invested heavily in this area have a clear and consistent brand identity that spans their online and offline channels, from seasonal appeal leaflets to their social media channels.

A *re*brand, of course, is a reimagining of all of this.

In some instances a rebrand can kick-start a conversation about building a new website, but let's say it's the other way around. What you'll need to do is assess how fit for purpose your current logo and visual identity is, and what work needs to be done (hint: there will more than likely be work to do here). Here are a few key themes to explore:

Is your brand identity fit for purpose?

Sometimes, old logos can carry a history, and therefore a lot of equity and shouldn't be disposed of without due consideration. But in many cases, older logos either need dramatically updating or putting in the bin. This is because the platforms which act as vehicles for your brand have changed massively in recent years, largely due to technological advancements. Your logo needs to be significantly more flexible than it used to, working in a range of contexts from your website and social media channels, to high-resolution screens and online videos. This puts a lot of demand on the logo to take different shapes, sizes and formats whilst still communicating effectively; something that older logos usually fail to do.

You can't teach an old dog new tricks. The same can be said for cheap or poorly-made logos.

I focus on the logo here because usually it's the first "thing" that people want to talk about when discussing brand. But in what other ways might your identity be unfit for purpose? I once spoke with an organisation who wanted to connect with a wider audience, but their website made heavy use of some very technical language that only the most passionate of supporters would understand. It completely lacked appeal to everyday or would-be supporters. Spend some time reviewing your entire brand platform: your logo, tone of voice, messaging, choice of imagery and all the rest to determine how effective, or otherwise, it might be. A great way to begin exploring this would be to create donor personas, which I cover in Chapter 8.

Which comes first: the website or the rebrand?

If you decide to update your brand identity, it's a good idea to do it *before* starting a new website project. This is because the website style will be heavily informed by the brand identity you create. The website designer will pick key colours from your brand identity, as well as typefaces (aka fonts) and imagery to get the tone just right. If you have yet to go through this process, I advise that you do so, as it can establish a unique image for your charity that helps to make you distinct and memorable. Once this is in place, use the new visual identity to influence the website style.

The logo design process

If there is one piece of design work that I wish were not so subjective, it would be the logo. The logo is the identifying mark of any organisation, and therefore everybody wants a say in what that looks like. This presents a real challenge for logo designers, because they need to integrate the ideas of a number of people whilst still reflecting the organisation as a whole. A less confident designer will produce a logo that pleases the stakeholders but looks a terrible mess that fails to communicate to the outside, or a relatively nice piece of work that nobody internally is happy with. You can see where the sweet spot is, but hopefully appreciate how challenging it is to achieve.

A key lesson that I have learned from working with logo designers in the past, and one that I hope to pass on to you, is to give the designer a *vision* and let them work their magic. Quite often, the stakeholder's instinct is to be prescriptive, and even sketch out the logo they would like to have made. But this misses the point of buying in expertise. Instead, describe your values and audience to the designer, and they will produce something wonderful that reflects your organisation in ways that you had not considered.

How much does a logo and brand identity cost?

As with the website design process it's tricky to put a figure on this. This is partly because the logo design market is wide, but the level of depth you need also varies. A logo designer might quote you a few thousand pounds, and this will give you a heavily involved process that results in an entire brand identity (logo, business card designs, social media graphics; the whole shebang). At the other end of the spectrum, you can buy a logo online for $30. Much like the web design process, it's important to go into any transaction with an open mind. Don't be afraid to negotiate on price, and as a rule of thumb, don't try to get it done on the cheap either. Your organisation is worth more than this.

What makes a good logo?

Much can be said about what constitutes a "good" logo. But the truth is that in reality the logo has one job: to communicate. You may not be a global consumer brand, I get that, but the rules of good logo design should still be observed:

A good logo is simple

A strong visual identity relies on clarity. No visual noise. Ideally, your logo will consist of only a few elements and not much text. In design, it's tempting to keep adding things - more colour, more text - but most often it is the act of *taking things away* that is key to an effective outcome.

A good logo is multipurpose

As alluded to earlier: logos need to work hard in whatever context you put them. A strong identity relies on your logo working across mediums to communicate your message clearly, and scaling to any size without loss of meaning. Think about your logo on the side of a bus as well as in an Instagram post or TikTok video.

A good logo reflects who you are

A branding specialist might ask you to describe your organisation using adjectives, such as "innovative" or "optimistic". A more wild approach might involve the old classic *if your organisation was a song, what song would it be?* The point here is to understand the driving ethos of your charity to tease out who you really are. This knowledge is captured and then represented in your visual identity and crucially, your logo.

So, do you need to rebrand?

I cannot answer this for you but would encourage you to hold a few internal discussions focused around the following points:

- Is our current brand identity comprehensive, or is it very basic?

- When did we last audit our brand identity?

- As an organisation, how much do we *value* our appearance?

  By exploring some of these talking points you can decide what work needs to be done.

Did you know?

You probably won't have heard the name Carolyn Davidson, but in 1971 she designed the Nike "Swoosh" logo, one of the most recognised logos in the world. She was paid $35 for it.[3]

Don't worry, a few years after Nike went public Davidson was given shares in the company that speculatively amounted to $1m. This goes some way to illustrate that design, much like art, is not just subjective in appeal but in every other measurable way as well.

---

[3] https://en.wikipedia.org/wiki/Carolyn_Davidson

Chapter 3:
PLANNING YOUR PROJECT

The planning process is where you begin to make your first big decisions about the project. Up until now, your project has been mostly theoretical. Now is the time to begin putting your ideas into action.

Assembling your team

If you work for a small charity it's quite likely that the very notion of having a "team" is entertaining. You may be solely responsible for various projects and find yourself short on time and resources. If this sounds like you, kudos for taking the time to read this book!

But delivering an effective website - one that will propel your organisation forward and stand the test of time - requires a few key roles to be fulfilled. For brevity, we'll outline the ideal team here and delve into more detail as we go. Bear in mind once again that one person may take on multiple roles.

Role	Responsibilities
Project manager	Manage project scope, people, timescales and delivery
Website developer	Design and build the website
Content writer	Produce key messages and content for the website
Marketing manager	Produce and execute a marketing strategy for the website

This list is by no means exhaustive; it is what I consider to be the "core team". Who in your team fits the bill for each of these roles? Let's take a look at each in a little more detail:

Project manager

The project manager (PM) is the overseer of the whole endeavour. It is their responsibility to ensure that the team has the tools, resources and knowledge they need to deliver a great website that does what it set out to do, in time and on budget. The PM must be assertive and adept at conflict resolution because a project which is inherently about *design* is subjective. Everybody has their own view on what looks and feels right, and opinions can vary greatly on this. A PM must negotiate these political obstacles and help the team settle on an equitable solution that doesn't harm the project. Finally, the PM will manage input from all stakeholders from trustees to end-users, and ensure that this gets fed back into the project development plan. No pressure, then.

Website developer

The role of the website developer, or website development team, is ultimately to deliver the website that you want. They will be acting under your instruction but should bring to the table their advice and expertise to assist you in making the best, most informed decisions. At times, the developer may even challenge your wishes if he or she believes the project would benefit. Alongside delivering the website to your specification, the developer should take responsibility for ensuring the website is accessible (i.e. it functions well on various devices and for those with disabilities) and is suitably constructed as to make it simple for you to maintain yourself. The developer may include training on how to do this, and you should enquire as to whether this is applicable when engaging an external supplier.

Content writer

Content writers are the lynchpin of the whole operation. Often, the content writer is also the project or marketing manager, and is responsible for putting together the overarching strategy behind the organisation's core messages. Without content, it is almost impossible to put together an effective website.

Working closely with the website developer, the content writer will produce text for website pages. This often includes introduction text (sometimes called "snippets" or "excerpts" which gives an overview of the page in question) as well as paragraphs of content.

In order to produce content, the writer, working with the marketing manager may include others internal and external to the organisation. For example, in order to obtain funding, your charity might produce case studies to demonstrate impact. In this instance the content writer might conduct interviews with internal staff and service users to collate this content and turn it into case studies for the website.

Marketing manager

As outlined above, the marketing manager may also be the content writer and/or the project manager. It is not unusual for multiple hats to be worn. But the role of marketing is distinct in that this person will be challenged with thinking about how the website fits into a wider marketing plan. How do you build excitement for the website launch? Which messages will be published on social media? How do you collect and manage data? What content will you publish on the website over the next 12 months?

These seem like big questions but building a marketing strategy around the website is essential. It can be light touch or in-depth, but the marketing manager's role is to determine what these activities look like and how they might be measured.

Defining your requirements

When planning your project you will typically produce a set of documents that outline the overall vision. It's important not to get too prescriptive at this point, and be open to suggestions and changes. Having said that, it is useful to note down non-negotiable requirements for the website alongside any "nice to haves"; budget and resource allowing.

I personally find that when embarking on a new website project, starting with a brainstorm session is a very positive approach. Think of it as a blank canvas. Take the largest piece of paper you can find, or ideally a whiteboard, and simply write down your ideas freely and without hesitation. You can do this on your own or with your team. If you're struggling to think up any ideas, it helps to check out what others are doing in your sector. Look at their websites, social media channels, newsletters and anything else you can find.

Note down the things you like (and if appropriate, the things you don't like!) on the paper. Discuss your work with your team and begin to refine it: which parts are top-priority? Which ideas can be implemented later, or scratched out completely?

This process helps to clarify two core areas of your project: your brief document and sitemap.

Brief document

Your brief will outline the goals of the project including the preferred timescales and budget. You don't need to go into a huge amount of detail at this stage because your chosen web developer should be able to offer advice and guidance, and answer any questions you might have. The key reasons for writing a brief is that it sets out and formalises your ideas in such a way that they can be clearly interpreted by your colleagues and suppliers. It also helps to ground the project in reality once you have this tangible asset in place.

To help you get started with putting your thoughts down on paper, I have produced an example website design brief for you to use here: http://bit.ly/34YN0Ak

Sitemap

A sitemap essentially illustrates the pages and sections on your website and defines how they link together. It helps you to understand the hierarchy of your pages, as well as any similarities between content. Think of it as getting a birds-eye view of your site as a whole. If you followed the brainstorming session described previously, it's likely you'll have already discovered many of the pages your new website needs to include. A sitemap enables you to give this some context, here's a basic example:

Example Project

About Us	Our Work	Support Us	News	Resources
Staff and Trustees	Case Studies	Donate	Subscribe	Research
Volunteers	Testimonials	Volunteer	Our Blog	Training
How to Volunteer	Get Involved	Appeals		Fundraising Kit
	Corporate Partners			
	Fundraising Events			
	Subscribe			

Created free using https://www.gloomaps.com

You can see how the content flows from top-level (i.e. Our Work) all the way down (i.e. Corporate Partners). Generally speaking, the top-level content is what you deem to be the most important, with lower-level content being a few clicks away and not immediately visible to your visitor (unless they entered the website on that section).

At this stage, it can be helpful to think about your stakeholders; the people who will use your website and who have a vested interest in your organisation. This book discusses two ways to do this: in Chapter 8 we cover persona development to help you understand the motivations of your users, or you may see Chapter 15 for a case study on co-creation: the process of designing a service *alongside* your users.

How will your website be built?

During the process of planning your website, you will likely begin to ask questions about how you're actually going to make it happen. I am going to cover three options here that will hopefully help you to formulate the best decision for your particular situation: using a pro bono designer, building the website yourself, or buying in a design service.

Using a pro bono web designer

Third sector organisations often get the opportunity to benefit from professional services delivered on a pro bono, free of charge basis.

For website design, I'm sorry to say this is typically a bad idea.

Allow me to explain why, and please know that I am in no way cynically trying to influence your view on this to benefit my own position as a web design service provider. Indeed, it is precisely *because* I work in this industry that I can explain to you why pro bono services usually don't cut the mustard. Pro bono services work best when:

- The project has fixed parameters (time, scope, and cost)
- The project is self-contained and has a clear end.

For website projects, neither of these things are true.

Consider that when you start the project, you know the least about it. You learn and evolve the requirements as you go. This can impact deadlines, scope and budget, and a pro bono provider with the best will in the world isn't going to continue to deliver against a project that has moving goalposts.

Websites are also never finished. Once you launch, you are going to need support, ad-hoc development work, hosting and maintenance. Is your pro bono supplier going to be there for this? Will they continue to deliver free of charge, or place a premium on their time?

Now, I *have* delivered pro bono websites in the past but it is something I choose to do very selectively, with clear parameters and with eyes wide open. Here is my advice if you choose to seek a pro bono website developer:

Find the right partner

Speak with your potential supplier and try to understand what is motivating them to do this for free. What are *their* goals? What are their values, and do they align with your own? Resist the urge to go all-in on the first provider who comes along who's waving the free flag.

Treat it like a paid project

Just because money isn't changing hands, both parties should behave as though it is. A supplier does not have the right to overreach in their role, and you should not let the project get deprioritised. Be professional. Sign contracts, agree deadlines, set conditions. Any sense that the project is worth *less* will result in disaster.

Be clear about everything

Make an effort to be as clear as possible about what needs to be delivered. Enquire about follow up support and services, and remove as much ambiguity as you can.

Pro bono services *can* deliver, but a fastidious approach must be deployed. What you save in money might come at the expense of delivery time or overall quality of service. Remember the project management triangle we discussed earlier?

Build the website yourself

Thanks to the march of progress within the web technology industry, it is now simple and cheap for anyone to put together a website, on their own and with no coding skills.

This is to be commended; it has lowered the barrier to entry onto the web as a creator and has helped to democratise the production and consumption of content. A cancer patient can share their journey on their own blog, a student can make and sell jewellery through an online store and independent journalists can shape the political conversation in ways never seen before.

But website design is still a profession, and like all professions it requires a level of experience, knowledge and skill to be seriously impactful. Understanding how to structure the flow of your content, developing visitor journeys, measuring performance and identifying key goals are all necessary steps to success that come with (sometimes bitter) experience.

If you are considering building your own website using a system like Squarespace or Wix, I encourage you to explore this option. For organisations who require only a minimal online presence and basic support, it may very well serve your needs.

I hope, however, that your ambitions are greater than this. A website is a big part of the supporter experience and it influences greatly how you are perceived from all sides. A well-considered website is far more likely to convince funders to work with you. I've heard on multiple occasions from charities who see their existing website as a "blocker to funding". Quite often, the website they are looking to have replaced is a "stop-gap" that somebody put together three years ago using a do-it-yourself website builder.

On top of this, the average website visitor is now more sophisticated, having become accustomed to slick, fast and easy to use websites thanks to the considerable investment in major social media platforms and mobile applications. Enlisting professional expertise to develop and support you will undoubtedly result in a more effective website and better all-round asset for your organisation. It can cost more, but the investment is almost always worth it.

Buying in a design service

Earlier, we outlined the challenges faced by those looking to enlist the help of a professional website designer. The market is wild and free, and you'll likely struggle to know where to begin if this if your first time working on a project like this. It is probably not worth me labouring the point here that I absolutely think you *should* buy in professional expertise, so let me offer you some guidance on how you might go about doing this successfully.

Word of mouth recommendations

Be sure to tap into your networks to find people who've been through this process before. Contact your partner organisations, ask on LinkedIn, phone up old colleagues; start by seeking a word of mouth recommendation to try and find a trusted supplier.

Tap into specialist networks

There are some fantastic online communities offering a wealth of advice that you can tap into. CharityConnect.co.uk is a forum for linking up third sector organisations, and Fundraising Chat, a private Facebook group, is brimming over with genuinely useful discussion on all aspects of working in charities. Don't be afraid to ask for supplier recommendations in these communities.

Search Google for local suppliers

Most of my customers are remote, and thanks to modern technology, communicating with them is easy. But I would be lying if I said that the strongest relationships aren't built on face to face interactions. Search Google for website developers specifically in your area.

After following the steps in this chapter, you will have established the roles and responsibilities of your core team, produced a basic project plan in the form of a brief and sitemap, and you will have hopefully decided how you want the website to be built. Great! It's now time to delve into some of the more technical aspects of your project.

Chapter 4:
CHOOSING A CMS

The acronym CMS stands for Content Management System, and this is the platform on which your website will be built. You're going to want to have control over updating your website without having a technical developer on hand, and the most common software used for this purpose is WordPress. WordPress was first released in 2003 under General Public License, which means the software is free to use, modify, copy or extend for any purpose. This is commonly called *open source software*, and open source is great because:

- You don't pay for the core software

- It can be extended using add-ons called plugins (however, many plugins also feature upgrades which have associated fees)

- It is supported by a global community of developers who contribute to its development

- If you're unhappy with your current provider, you can easily find another who will also have expertise in the same software

- Much of the "heavy lifting" is already done for you, so setting up a feature-rich website using open source software is considerably cheaper and quicker than producing a custom solution from scratch.

I really like the ethos of open-source software; it speaks to my inner-socialist. The idea of a worldwide team contributing to the development of a platform which can be used, at its base level for free, has empowered both individuals and organisations of all sizes to do great things. The reason for my emphatic support for open source is, in part, to inspire you to learn more about it, but also to illustrate that it's often the most pragmatic approach as well.

WordPress vs other solutions

Whilst this section is titled "Choosing a CMS", I'm going to go all-in and throw my weight behind using WordPress for your CMS. In the interest of balance, however, I'm going to talk you through a few other options to equip you with the knowledge that you need should an alternative solution be suggested to you.

WordPress vs Drupal

Drupal will be forever in my heart as I have spent a great deal of time working with it over the years. Drupal, like WordPress, is an open-source CMS that is supported by a global community. Its usage is significantly lower than WordPress, however, and this is because its learning curve is notably higher. Drupal is arguably the more powerful of the two, and developers are more drawn to it thanks to the elegance of its "node" based architecture. I won't go any further into this, but in my opinion, Drupal is more developer-friendly at the cost of its editor experience. Updating content on a WordPress site is generally very simple, but Drupal can be more challenging as content editing can lead to a game of hide-and-seek that will have you on the phone to your developer to find out how to make the smallest of amends. Drupal, as a CMS, is favoured by very large, high-traffic websites operated by technical content editors. As most small organisations don't fit this bill, WordPress would be my preferred choice for ease of use and low barrier to entry.

WordPress vs Joomla

Joomla is another popular open-source web development platform. My knowledge of this piece of software is not as extensive, but in my experience it falls into the same "trap" as Drupal in that developers find themselves more at home using it than website editors. It, too, has a far smaller user base than WordPress. If a provider offers you Joomla, be sure to inquire about ease-of-use and understand their motivation for suggesting this platform.

WordPress vs an in-house solution

A goal of some design companies is to build their own in-house platform that they can sell to their clients, typically on a subscription basis. There are some good reasons for this: they will know the software inside out so can resolve technical issues quickly, and it can be tailored to do exactly what you need and nothing more.

However, there are also plenty of reasons to be sceptical: a proprietary solution will lock you into one provider, and moving away could be costly or even impossible. Because of this, you may be subject to price hikes over time, and you'll be reliant on one company for support. And frankly, in my experience in-house solutions rarely stack up against the leading open source solutions in terms of features, flexibility and future-proofing. In-house and proprietary solutions carry risks; be absolutely certain it is the right path for you before taking it. See "The fallacy of the all-in-one solution" in Chapter 10 for further reading.

Did you know?

WordPress began life as a blogging platform - essentially a way to keep an online diary - but as its popularity grew pressure mounted on the development community to expand its capability into a full website builder. Today, almost 35% of all websites are built on WordPress[4], powering sites for household names such as Usain Bolt, Beyonce and The Rolling Stones, as well a global consumer brands such as Mercedes-Benz and Sony Music.

---

[4] https://kinsta.com/wordpress-market-share/

What to look for in a WordPress developer

Whichever website platform you choose, it's important to understand what you're actually going to get from your provider. Here's a little industry nugget for you: a CMS is only as good as the developer who configures it. Though your brief might clearly state the need for "a website that is easy to manage", this can mean something very different to others. I've seen cases where content *can* be fully managed, but the CMS has been configured in such a way that one must jump through a number of quite dangerous-looking hoops to make any changes. As one client told me of her current website, "I don't even dare to change the homepage". This is not the outcome we are looking for.

It's important, therefore, to outline your requirements and have the conversation early on. Here are a few questions you can ask your provider to help that conversation along:

Will you buy a theme and customise it, or build one for us?

In the open-source CMS world, a "theme" refers to the look and feel of the website. There is an enormous market of thousands of readymade themes that can be bought for around $50 and then minimally customised to meet your needs. A developer might do this for you if you are very tight on budget and need something up and running quickly, with minimal fuss. The downside, of course, is that an "off the shelf" theme can only go so far in truly reflecting your organisation. In my experience and professional opinion, a readymade theme is rarely a long-term solution. A better option is to design and build a theme to meet your needs. In practice this means that you'll be leveraging a CMS like WordPress for its back-end functionality, but the customer-facing front-end will be tailored to your organisation.

Will you host with WordPress.com?

Hosting, in short, is the place where your website lives on the internet, and one of the reasons that WordPress reached such dizzying heights of popularity is because the company offers a hosted version of it. If you head over to wordpress.com you'll see that you can sign up there and then to use WordPress immediately. There are a few benefits to this: security, backups and basic maintenance are in place automatically, and the monthly cost is modest. However, many developers will be reluctant for you to go this route, and I'm totally with them on the reasons why. In short, when you host your WordPress website on wordpress.com developers are very limited in what they can actually do with it. Want extra plugins to extend the website and build additional functionality? Unlikely. Need some custom code writing? Forget about it. Much like the example above where I talk about a readymade theme, hosting with wordpress.com carries limitations that any serious organisation will grow out of very quickly.

The better and more standardised approach is for developers to download a complete copy of WordPress and install it on their own web server. Because this provides a more configurable environment, they will be able to build you a more robust and customised website. Therefore, any WordPress provider should be offering you a *self-hosted* version of the CMS, and *not* one hosted on wordpress.com.

What maintenance will you provide?

As we have just covered, a self-hosted version of any open-source software such as WordPress will need some sort of monthly maintenance package to keep it in shape. This is very important; open-source platforms are updated frequently, and are constantly in the crosshair of hackers due to the sheer volume of websites they power. Many developers are happy to hand over the website and walk away, but more savvy providers know that there is great mutual value to be found in providing ongoing maintenance. This could include daily backups, security upgrades, technical support and minor changes to your website itself. Often referred to as a "service level agreement", this is a legally-binding contract that stipulates in detail what your provider will and won't do for you after website launch.

Maintaining a relationship with your supplier is useful for other reasons as well: I have seen first-hand companies who have undergone cyber-attacks to be left in want of a proverbial paddle. Administrators locked out of websites. Data being stolen and entire websites taken offline. This is a nightmare scenario for any organisation. It has operational and legal implications, and a light-touch service level agreement with a good web developer can avert disaster and assist in times of need.

Be sure to speak with your supplier about a basic maintenance agreement early on in the process, and if possible agree what it might cover so you have some assurance going forward.

A word about privacy

I've heard on more than a couple of occasions that some charities expect leniency, or even exemption from privacy crackdowns like the GDPR introduced in 2018. This is not the case, and you should observe ICO policy[5] on how best to deal with handling data responsibly. When looked at through the prism of positivity, GDPR becomes a good thing because it ensures that your data is clean and up to date.

---

[5] https://ico.org.uk/for-organisations/in-your-sector/charity/

What training will you provide?

If you're not used to managing websites and have never used a Content Management System like WordPress before, it's likely that you will need some basic training on how to get the best out of it. In most instances, managing content will be fairly self-explanatory, but it is worth enquiring with your chosen provider to find out what training and support they can offer you.

In this chapter I have advocated the use of open-source software, and WordPress in particular. These tools provide the platform for content management, but shortly we will see why a dynamic content strategy is crucial to your online success.

Chapter 5:
PRODUCING EFFECTIVE CONTENT

Earlier I touched on the role of the content writer. Here, I want to expand on the importance of it, and on the vitality of well-considered content in general.

The content writer really is the engine in the creative process, because the content is the tangible "thing" that website visitors consume. In a way, all other roles exist to facilitate this one; the website designer makes the content look attractive and engaging, and the comms manager uses it in marketing materials. Content can make or break a website, marketing campaign, or any other vehicle used to deliver a message, for it is the *message* that is paramount.

A multi-purpose content strategy

I'll discuss the content production process shortly, but in the meantime here is a flavour of some common types of content that will hopefully stoke up some ideas within your own team:

Blog posts

Perhaps the most common piece of content on the web is the humble blog post. A blog post is a piece of text content, usually around 500-1000 words, that tends to cover a single topic. Recently won a funding bid? Write a blog post to announce it. Want to share your best practices? Write a top 10 list. Taken on a new member of staff? Allow them to introduce themselves on the blog. Your blog tells the chronological story of your organisation, demonstrating to supporters and potential funders what you've been up to. Aim to produce content for your blog regularly, and you'll soon build up a timeline of content that you can reference time and again.

Podcasts/video

Thanks to internet streaming platforms and improvements in mobile technology over the past decade, it is now easy to produce basic video and audio content for the web. Podcasting in the third sector has increased greatly over the last few years, as charities realise it is a cost-effective way to reach their target audience. Video and podcast content provides a different, richer medium for your organisation to get the message out to your community. It serves as an engaging and accessible way to reach new supporters as well as nurture relationships with existing ones. Often, media content like this can also be transcribed into blog posts in the format of interviews and opinion pieces, enabling you to squeeze even more value from it. If you've yet to delve into the world of podcasting, take a look at the website anchor.fm to set up your first podcast for free.

Case studies

Like blog posts, case studies and success stories are cornerstones of the successful charity website. They are the best way to convert passers-by into supporters and convince potential funders that your organisation is worth investing in. A good case study feeds into your theory of change and wider impact aspirations. Be sure to spend the time developing case study material for your website and marketing channels. Seek testimonials from service users and supporters, use facts and figures to demonstrate impact and tell compelling stories that create an emotional connection with readers.

FAQs

Even if your charity is small, it is likely that donors or service users will have questions before they engage with you. FAQs (Frequently Asked Questions) provide a space to proactively answer their questions and concerns. For extra impact include a call to action. For example, if one question is "how will you spend my donation", take the time to explain this carefully and then ask for support.

Infographics

An infographic (a compound of the words "information" and "graphic") is a way to make traditionally complex or dry subjects engaging by graphically illustrating them. Infographics often include numbers and charts designed in such a way to make them easy to interpret, referred to as *data visualisation*. With the advent of online video, the heyday of the infographic has now passed, but the idea of data visualisation isn't going anywhere. If your charity seeks to get across complex information in a simple, cost-effective and visually-striking way, creating infographics can still be a way to achieve this. Canva.com is a great way to get started with this.

Content is still king

You may have heard the old adage that "content is king", and in 2020 it truly still is. The key point to consider is that your content should now be richer, taking the form of written text, images, audio and video, and repackaged to suit its context. For example, an appeal video on your website might be 3 minutes long, but the same message could be recut for Twitter and reduced to 30 seconds (more suited to a passive, scrolling audience). It is critical that your charity understands the importance and vitality of good, relevant content. Once this has been fully appreciated, a world of possibility opens up and you can breathe new life into your organisation through content production.

How to produce content that clicks

The problem that so many businesses and non-profit organisations have is that they're not daring enough with the content they produce. The web is an ocean of very similar content, and most of it really quite boring. It makes sense when you think about it: many organisations serve the same people, in much the same way, and therefore their messaging and marketing materials are all quite similar. Not a great deal of *imagination* goes into creating anything new, as organisations basically copy each other. The result is a string of duplicated content that really does nothing to engage readers and as such, is ineffective as a marketing tool.

This needs to change.

It's already incredibly difficult to be heard online, simply because there is so much *stuff* competing for our attention. In this section I'd like to share with you some ways to help you to be bold, and produce content that clicks.

#1 What is unique about you?

Every individual has something unique about them, so without doubt every organisation does as well. I'm not talking about some unique characteristic or talent (though you could very well tap into that); I'm talking about your *story*. Every member of your team, including you reading this right now, has experience that nobody else has. Don't fall into the trap of thinking "nobody cares about what I have to say" because in reality, you most likely have a huge amount of informative, entertaining or otherwise valuable experience to share. Here are a few nuggets to get you started:

When, how and why did your organisation come into being?

Your story is more valuable to your supporters than you realise. Does your charity have a history going back generations? Talk about how times have changed. Are you based in an interesting building? Share its heritage. What's your organisation's guiding mission? Remember, people don't buy *what* you do; they buy *why* you do it. This was argued brilliantly in the 2009 book *Start With Why* by Simon Sinek, which I recommend all non-profit organisations read.

What idiosyncrasies do you have?

Each organisation has its own unique complexion. Perhaps you have an eccentric volunteer who doesn't mind putting themselves out there to support you, or some celebrity patron who would be happy to engage in video or podcast content. Perhaps a member of staff is prolific within a specific or quirky niche. How can you tap into these resources? When you start seeing the value in everything around you, you realise just how much potential there is.

What actually makes you different?

This is a troublesome question for all organisations and many struggle to answer it, particularly in the early days. Humans are social creatures and we tend to learn from and follow others. But over time, you develop your own way of seeing and doing things. What makes the way that you deliver your service different from everybody else? How have you diverged from the group? Meditate on this question, and if you can't answer it, perhaps your organisation has yet to establish its identity and a little more growth is required. This will come with time; keep going.

#2 Can you create something unique?

As stated earlier, so many organisations say the same thing, just in slightly different ways. Can you turn this on its head? Take note of the common approach that others in your sector take. Examine the similarities, and think about how you can offer something original. This makes you more memorable and interesting, and helps your messaging to stand out from the crowd.

An interesting example of this is Crohn's & Colitis UK, a charity fighting inflammatory bowel disease. This is a condition that affects over 300,000 people in the UK, and can be difficult to explain to those who don't experience its symptoms. The charity, along with providing general information about the condition, created a mobile app called In My Shoes[6] that gives friends and loved-ones of sufferers the chance to experience what it might be like for 24 hours. This helps to build awareness and creates understanding and empathy for those with the condition. From a marketing perspective, it puts Crohn's & Colitis UK way ahead of the game because they didn't simply fall back on offering the same information about the condition that can be found anywhere else; they created something unique.

#3 What does your audience want?

To write content that clicks with your readers you're going to have to understand what they want from you. We cover persona development in Chapter 8 that will help you to break this down, but as a rule of thumb always consider your reader when writing content. Read your words back - do you feel bored? Rewrite it. Do you cover the key points or is there too much fluff? Cut it down. If it helps, ask your colleagues to read your content and provide honest feedback. The trick here is to write content *intentionally*; so many of us switch onto autopilot when writing and it makes for a lacklustre read.

---

[6] https://www.ittakesguts.org.uk/share/in-my-shoes-app

Going viral: the ice bucket challenge

Back in the summer of 2014, the internet was awash, almost literally, with videos of people throwing buckets of water over themselves. Why? Because of the ALS Ice Bucket Challenge.

You'll almost certainly have seen the videos. The idea was to throw the water over yourself, then nominate three friends to do the same. Everybody involved donated money to a charity focusing on ALS (known as motor neurone disease in the UK).

In just a few weeks over the summer period, people shared over 1.2 million videos on Facebook and mentioned the challenge more than 2.2 million times on Twitter. This yielded a massive $41.8 million in donations from 739,000 new donors, resulting in research that successfully identified a third gene that causes the disease.[7]

This is an example of the amazing power of viral content, and in particular video that incorporates people putting themselves out there for a good cause. What interesting video content can you or your supporters to create?

---

[7] https://edition.cnn.com/2016/07/27/health/als-ice-bucket-challenge-funds-breakthrough/index.html

In this chapter I have explained why content is so fundamental to your website and comms strategy. Along with the practicalities of actually producing content, I have also covered some key methods you can use to tap into your organisation's story and develop content that truly reflects who you are and engages your audience. In the next chapter, we'll be looking at how to produce content that raises your profile in search engines like Google.

Chapter 6:
OPTIMISING FOR SEARCH ENGINES

You will have probably come across the acronym SEO at some point. This stands for Search Engine Optimisation and it is a loose term that describes how "findable" your website is in search engines like Google. Search engines are the single biggest source of website traffic on the web, with Google claiming the top spot. Because so many people use Google to search the web, you can probably appreciate how competitive it is getting on that first page of results. In essence, the practice of SEO is about achieving this.

SEO considerations when building a new website

If your organisation has been around for some time, or is recognised as an authority within your sector, putting a new website in place will probably require additional considerations in terms of SEO. It is not unusual for websites with a long history to have acquired a lot of what we call "link equity". Link equity essentially refers to the number of websites that link to yours. In short, if this number is high it means that your website is popular! It means that competing organisations look up to you, journalists and researchers cite your work and you have a healthy range of marketing activities and channels. These activities create a "buzz" around your organisation, which means that people are talking about you. You may be referenced on corporate fundraising blogs, in research papers, the local press and so forth. Each time a page on your website is referenced by one of these external sources, it builds your website's authority and this is the de facto measure by which your website is ranked in Google. If you want to be on page one of Google, you need other websites to link to yours.

There are most likely a number of websites out there that already link to you, so when building a new website, you'll need to analyse your current website to find out who's linking to you and what pages they are referencing. This is important, because neglecting to do this could damage your link equity, which in turn will destroy your search engine rankings leading to a significant drop in web traffic. If you currently *don't* rely on search engines to send you visitors, it is still worth going through this process, albeit without the same sense of urgency.

How to conduct a backlink analysis

A backlink is any link that points from another website to yours, as illustrated by the following diagram:

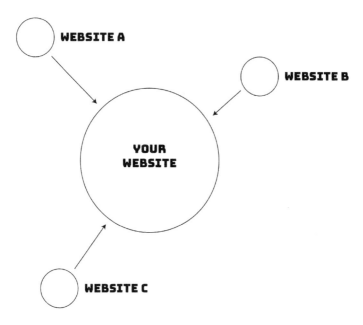

To conduct a backlink analysis you're going to want to look at your analytics tool (probably Google Analytics) under "referrers". Spend some time here looking at the places that are sending traffic and make a note of which pages they are linking to. It is worth pointing out that this is the job of the website developer or marketing manager, and should be considered a significant part of the project. Especially if your existing website is of high current value, do not skip this step.

Once you have listed out all the popular pages that you know people are linking to, your new website must either:

1. Replicate these pages, at the same location or,
2. Redirect to new pages, at new locations.

Let's look at an example:

On your current website, let's imagine you have a page that features some research into the mental wellbeing of students, and other websites are linking to it. This page can be found at *yourwebsite.com/papers/research/student-wellbeing*. When it comes to building your new website, you need to consider what will happen to this page. You will probably wish to keep it, but in all likelihood it will be placed elsewhere within the site as new decisions are made about structure, navigation and so on. Let's say you no longer have a section at *papers/research* and you wish to publish this under a new *insights* section instead. If you go ahead and do this, anybody trying to visit the existing page will be met with a 404 error, which means the page no longer exists, because it will have been moved from that location.

Before your new website launches, you need to create a set of 301 redirects, which inform search engines that a page has been permanently moved to a new location. Therefore, in this example, your redirect will look like this:

*website.com/**papers/research**/student-wellbeing -> website.com/**insights**/student-wellbeing*

This requires a level of technical know-how to pull off but is certainly worth exploring *before* you launch a new website. Be sure to raise this with your website developer.

A quicker backlink overview

To help you conduct a backlink analysis take a look at https://ahrefs.com/backlink-checker. Enter your website address, and the free version of this tool will return a sample list of the websites currently referencing yours. If you're struggling to use your analytics software, or simply don't have any, this could be a better place to start.

Taking SEO further

If you've been involved in a digital marketing project previously, you'll no doubt be well acquainted with the importance of ranking well in search engines. We've looked at how you can capitalise on existing SEO value, but how do you actually *do* SEO?

SEO is something of a rabbit hole; a tunnel of twists and opportunities, but often navigated in the dark! To execute a successful SEO strategy you'll need to understand that the practice is both a science and an art. This can sound a little scary, but the fact is that all marketing is a science in that different methods must be trialled before a satisfactory outcome is produced. SEO is no different, and you'll do well to adopt an experimental attitude before investing any significant funds.

Preparing your website for SEO

There are some technical considerations to be aware of if you want to get serious about SEO. Your website developer should be able to advise on each of these topics, but knowing the terminology is always useful to help strengthen your position working with a supplier.

#1 The Google ecosystem

If you want to rank highly in Google, you have to play Google's game. At time of writing, the search engine accounts for 87% of all UK web searches.[8] The company is the world leader in search and provides a number of useful tools to help you do well:

Google Analytics

Google Analytics allows you to track visitor behaviour on your website. There are of course better tools on the market, but this one is free and pretty much the industry standard. It gives you basic information, such

---

[8] https://www.statista.com/statistics/280269/market-share-held-by-search-engines-in-the-united-kingdom/

as how many visitors you've received, how long they spent looking at your pages, and which are the most popular pages on your site.

Google Search Console
Search Console (previously called Webmaster Tools) allows you to get an inside view of your website from Google's perspective. For example, if your website is exhibiting any security errors or contains any broken links, you will be alerted and prompted to fix these issues. This is handy for keeping on top of the technical aspects of SEO.

Google My Business
If you work in your local area it is crucial to be listed in Google My Business. This enables your website to appear in local search results. It is free to get listed and can be done within a week. Moreover, having a verified physical address gives your website more oomph as it signals that your organisation is "real". Yes, even in this digital age it helps to have physical premises.

#2 Install an SSL certificate
An SSL (Secure Sockets Layer) certificate ensures that any information submitted on your website (such as a username and password) gets encrypted. This is simple and usually inexpensive, and is important from an SEO perspective because Google sometimes penalises websites that are not secure. If your website does not carry a valid SSL certificate, your chances of ranking highly in Google are diminished because the search

engine does not want to send its users to potentially untrustworthy or spurious websites. To see if your website currently has SSL installed, simply add an "s" to the URL, i.e. https://mywebsite.co.uk. If it works, and you see a small padlock icon, you're secure.

#3 Mobile friendliness

For similar reasons as outlined above, Google prefers to send its users to websites that are guaranteed to work on their chosen device. If your website is not "responsive" to different screen sizes, such as mobile phones, it is highly unlikely that Google will send you traffic from mobile phone users. This makes total sense, when you think about it; who would want to visit a website that works poorly on a mobile device if that is what they are currently using?

Defining your keywords

One of the first and most useful exercises to go through when thinking about SEO is to create a list of keywords and phrases that relate to your organisation and services. The trick here is to think about how other people might describe your services, and subsequently, how they might search for them online. Try to put yourself in their shoes and get creative!

Let's take a look at an example. Imagine that your charity provides temporary housing and rehabilitation for homeless ex-veterans in Nottingham. Your goal would be to think about the *search phrases* that people may use to locate a service like yours. It can be helpful, also, to consider the motivation for their search. Is somebody seeking you to make a referral, or are they simply a concerned member of the public who wishes to support ex-military personnel back into society?

Spend an hour with your team to write down all of your core services, and think of as many words and phrases that people may use to describe and locate these services. Here are a few ideas that you might think of:

- "Donate to homeless veterans Nottingham"
- "Help homeless ex-army Nottingham"
- "Support homeless vets in the midlands"

(Notice how I've used synonyms such as "help" and "support", as well as varied the noun to include "veterans", "vets" and "ex-army". Remember that people describe similar things in different ways!)

Once you've got this list of words, be sure to pepper them into the content you write on your website and social channels. The reason for doing this is twofold: by repeating the same messages it helps to establish your message in the minds of your readers, but it also tells search engines like Google what you're all about. This makes it easier to rank highly for the keywords and phrases that are most relevant to you.

Be careful not to sound too robotic when using keywords. It's very easy to slip into writing for search engines, and as such begin repeating your keywords so they read in an unnatural way. Steve Jobs of Apple famously said that "marketing is about values", so let your passion shine through and be genuine.

Setting up landing pages

A solid SEO strategy tends to include landing pages. A landing page is a page on your website dedicated to a single purpose. For example, your charity may work nationally to rehome abandoned animals, including cats and dogs as well as more exotic pets such as snakes and bearded dragons. Alongside rehoming, your charity also provides care and medical support to help animals transition into a new environment. Your charity is relatively large, working across the country delivering a wide range of services.

Landing pages enable you to slice and dice your service offering to speak more directly to different audiences. For example, you may choose to create a page on your website based around a specific location and subset of animals you rehome. Adding a page to your website titled *"Adopt a rescue dog in Edinburgh"* enables you to speak directly to the appropriate people: people seeking a rescue dog in Edinburgh. You may repeat this process by producing dozens of other narrowly-focused pages, which helps to develop many streams of targeted website visitors over time.

Moreover, landing pages tend to include a highly-relevant call to action, which can be effectively done because the audience is so targeted. In this case, you might actually include pictures of the animals currently looking to be rehomed and ask the reader to call a local number to book a visit.

Hopefully this demonstrates to you the potential for landing pages to earn you more relevant website traffic, and energise your visitors to take action. What services do you offer that could be turned into targeted landing pages?

Experimenting with SEO

It is beyond the scope of this book to advise in detail on the many aspects of SEO. What we have covered here should get you started and check a few best-practice boxes, but in reality you will want to spend some time experimenting with your content. Write blog posts of varying lengths and topics, and change up your keywords and phrases. Be sure to keep glancing at your web analytics to track what is gaining reader interest and what isn't. This is where SEO strays far from being an exact science more into the territory of artistic experimentation. With everything you do, think about how you are adding value to your reader: are you answering their questions? Entertaining them? Comforting them? You won't earn the trust and respect of the major search engines if you do not first achieve this with your readers.

Patience means prizes

The real secret to successful SEO - if such a thing exists - is being patient. Don't think of your search engine positioning as a "campaign" as it's more than that: it is an ongoing activity that you should work at consistently. Being successful in this arena is a test of your mettle and demonstrates how seriously you take market visibility in general. Have patience.

Chapter 7:
JOINING THE ONLINE CONVERSATION

Social media has something of a tarnished reputation these days due to the proliferation of spurious content, reports of fake users and various privacy issues. But these online communities also reflect some of the kinder aspects of humanity, connecting related groups, bridging geographical gaps and fostering genuine engagement between brands and end-users.

When we talk about social media, our minds tend to envisage the neverending feeds of Facebook, Twitter and LinkedIn. But this is simply the tip of the iceberg. In this chapter, I'd like to dig a little deeper into what social media could mean for your charity, how it can support your website, and go beyond the usual banal promotion tactics that so many organisations deploy (often to their dismay).

Discovering your tribe

The web is a sprawling network of loosely-joined communities that exist much deeper than the shiny surface of social media would have us believe. Scratch this surface and you'll find private Facebook groups, offbeat community forums and Subreddits, each one focusing on some niche topic and frequented by a relatively small number of dedicated followers. To make the most of social media, it is your job to uncover these communities and genuinely participate in them. Gone are the days of jumping onto Twitter and announcing your existence; the most effective marketers realise that unfortunately, nobody cares. The goal here is to add value to the discourse, and be rewarded for your contribution.

Using social media effectively

You should look at social media as conversations between people. When you frame it this way, the idea of seeing it simply as an advertising opportunity feels strange, doesn't it? And yet, so many companies and charities shout about their latest promotions and appeals to minimal effect. It is, of course, perfectly acceptable to advertise your service on social media, but know that this must be done in the context of an otherwise muted, value-added approach. Here are some methods that you can deploy in order to use social media more effectively:

Ask questions

Questions are conversation-starters and when asked delicately can prompt genuine discussion and debate. In this NSPCC example, the question can even be rhetorical; it is simply a tactic to produce engagement.

Engage with others

You don't need to wade into other people's conversations, but be sure to reply to those who mention you on social media. If somebody proudly announces their support for you on Facebook, it's common for the most effective organisations to thank that person publicly. Similarly, if somebody asks a question, make sure you answer it in good time. Social media is not simply a marketing channel; it is also a customer support line.

Use video

Videos can be an effective way to engage people and halt the passive scrolling through their endless social media feeds. Videos don't need to be polished or perfect, and can be filmed on most smartphones. Don't be afraid to show your face on camera to give your social media a unique and personal touch. Content might include informal chats with volunteers, a behind the scenes peek in your office, or a "vlog" (video log) of your day exhibiting at a conference.

Seek out the right people

In a nod to our earlier point about discovering your tribe, be sure to search for the right people to follow, places to join and discussions to take part in. This takes a bit of time, and means straying away from the main feeds. Search Facebook and LinkedIn for specific groups and individuals operating in your sector, search Google for niche communities and forums, and follow specific hashtags on all the major networks to be kept in the loop when something interesting happens.

Social media and your website

It's common to think of your website and your social platforms as one of the same, but they are in fact very different channels. By now, hopefully you recognise that social media is more a place where discussion happens, and where to spend time "warming up" prospective supporters. Your website, by contrast, is your opportunity to seal the deal. It is the platform on which to make your case for support, that lays out your stall and asks "would you like to help?"

The instinct to conflate these two worlds is unfortunately very strong. Just as we see people using social media solely to direct people to their website, there is also a tendency to smatter our websites with social media feeds. The networks themselves make this relatively easy by providing copy/paste code that drops their feeds directly into your web pages. I would ask you to think twice about doing this: not only are they frankly quite ugly but the audiences for these two vehicles - your website and your social media - are quite different. A better approach, in my opinion, is simply to link out to your social platforms rather than allowing their contents to spill over into your own website.

Should we recruit a social media volunteer?

There is sometimes a strange perception of social media. It is simultaneously seen as both vital and yet pointless. Difficult yet easy. This contradiction is probably born out of ignorance about strategy, cost and effectiveness, bumping up against the constant messages we all receive that using social media is critically important. Therefore it is not surprising that many organisations wish to delegate away their social media "problem". But because of scepticism on the effectiveness, they choose not to invest and instead seek volunteer support. Worse still, they look to recruit a young person (because all young people know how to "do social!") and they entrust this often-inexperienced intern with a significant comms channel. I'm not here to say that this is inherently a bad idea, but I would encourage you to plan a basic strategy, have desired outcomes and attempt to measure your social media activity. Don't allow delegation to become an abdication of responsibility; your social channels can be powerful components in your overall marketing plan, and so they should be respected and treated as such.

To truly get value from online communities you need to firstly *create* value. Followers must be earned. Think back to what we have covered so far when talking about content, and the different forms this can take: video, infographics and podcasts. How can you join the conversation?

Next up, we'll be taking a look at persona design, enabling you to define and communicate with your audience in a meaningful way.

Chapter 8:
DEFINING PERSONAS

In my experience, personas seem to be discussed more in the third sector than in the private sector. I feel that this hints at the generally more empathic nature of charities, and the deeper connection with service users, than what might typically be found in commercial enterprises. If you're not familiar with personas, think of them as a method by which you can understand your users in order to better serve them. A persona is the amalgamation of any research you've conducted with your target users, consolidated into one fictional person. A persona typically has a name and photograph, and some key information about them. You would then optimise your services in line with the expectations of your personas.

Creating a persona

The real value in creating personas comes from the process of reducing guesswork and working toward a deeper understanding of what your users actually need. You *can* make assumptions based on existing knowledge, but I encourage you to speak with your stakeholders to identify common concerns. This dialog could take the form of surveys and questionnaires, telephone interviews or real-world workshops where you hold group conversations to focus on what is important to your stakeholders. You would then draw themes from this data which would inform your persona design.

Let us imagine for a moment that you have surveyed a pool of donors to get their feedback on the donation process on your current website. Several participants hint that they were unsure how their donation was going to be used, but decided they trust your organisation enough to give their support anyway.

What can you learn from this? This is extremely valuable feedback, but how do you ensure that it gets acknowledged in your website project and more importantly, continues to be considered going forward? You create a persona! Let's look at a basic example of a persona that addresses this concern right now:

Photo by Kal Vusuals (http://unslpash.com)

Jemima, 27

Jemima supports a number of charitable causes, often raising money through events and makes monthly donations to a couple of local charities. She enjoys feeling like she is making a difference, and subscribes to a number of publications that cover causes she cares about.

Now, when developing donation areas on your website you would reference this persona to ensure that it addresses Jemima's needs. Key to this persona is not just the fact that Jemima supports charities, it is that she likes to *feel* like she is "making a difference". In practice, you would pepper your donation pages with case studies and stories that would engage Jemima and make her want to become a part of your work. This would encourage her to support you and in return she would feel her donation is having an impact. Note also that Jemima is clearly engaged in the third sector; subscribing to various industry publications. Can you partner with any relevant organisations to bolster trust in your charity? The goal here is to think about how you can build additional support from people like Jemima.

For a more in-depth view on persona development, see Chapter 15 for my interview with Vikram, a senior user experience designer.

How to use personas

The beauty of this approach is that you're not just targeting a woman called Jemima; you are addressing the concerns of a group of users in one go. The persona is simply a distillation of this group's concern into one, digestible business goal (*to ensure donors feel like they are making a difference*). Moreover, personas are business assets that can be used repeatedly moving forward. Let's imagine that your website launches and several months later you develop a new appeal. If you don't reference your personas you run the risk of once again failing to address the core needs of your users. Personas are there to remind you to keep your supporters at the heart of your comms which, when put into practice, could help to give your charity a serious competitive advantage.

Helping Latinos find cancer information using personas

The US National Cancer Institute (NCI) wanted to connect with Latino readers who were seeking healthcare services or information about cancer. The first port of call was to simply translate the existing English-speaking website into Spanish, but subsequent research found that this led to "cold" and "impersonal" language that failed to connect with Latino readers. To remedy this, the team at NCI conducted research to identify key values, beliefs, and language practices of Latino readers. From this they created 14 personas that could be used to reference the findings, and to speak more directly to Spanish-speaking readers across the service. How can you adapt this process to deliver something similar for your organisation?[9]

Much of what is discussed in this book focuses on serving the needs of the end-user, whether that is a service user, donor or even an internal stakeholder such as the editor of the website. Conducting research to turn into personas is probably the purest manifestation of this idea, often referred to as *user-centred design*, and it allows you to zero-in on what's really important. Most organisations don't bother doing this, instead

---

[9] https://digital.gov/2015/03/02/persona-development-case-study-nci-and-spanish-language-outreach/

acting on assumptions and guesswork. Personas give you the opportunity to forge deeper connections with stakeholders, leading to longer and more fruitful relationships.

Chapter 9:
BEING INCLUSIVE

Inclusivity in the context of website development is generally referred to as "accessibility". This is the practice of making sure that your website works for everyone, regardless of their ability, environment or chosen input device. The core functions that your website is designed to perform should operate in every reasonable situation. This is important, because one in five working-age adults in the UK are disabled[10], living with conditions that affect them physically or cognitively, impairing vision or hearing, or presenting motor problems that can affect how they use a mouse and keyboard. This, coupled with the astounding fact that 95% of charity websites fail to meet basic accessibility criteria[11], makes for a bleak experience if you're the one in five.

Digital accessibility in the real world

To help build a picture of just how prevalent inaccessibility is, consider the following fictional scenarios:

_____

[10] https://www.scope.org.uk/media/disability-facts-figures/
[11] https://resources.lloydsbank.com/pdf/bdi-report-2018.pdf

Steven tries to book a GP appointment

Steven, or Ste as he's more affectionately known, is on the phone to his local GP's practice. He's in a queue, and the recorded message tells him that he can find more information online, and even book an appointment, on the GP's website. Ste is 57 and doesn't own a laptop, but he does have an Android mobile phone (the one he's currently using to wait in the queue, as it happens). He hangs up the phone and opens his mobile's web browser to go to the doctor's website. He has used his phone to do all kinds of things recently; things he didn't even know were possible just a few years ago. He ordered flowers online for his wife, and booked a getaway for their anniversary. But the GP's website doesn't look quite right. For a start, much of the text is so small that he can barely read it, and some of the pictures seem to overlap important pieces of information that he needs to navigate the website. He manages to move around the website, but each page takes a long time to appear, and when he finally reaches the booking form he finds it too difficult to use and gives up. Back in the queue he goes.

What is happening here?

In this case it appears that the GP's website has not been made with mobile visitors in mind. Ste struggled to engage with the content because the text, written for much larger screens, was too small to read. The form fields were difficult to use on a small screen, and the layout meant it wasn't clear what information to enter into each box. On a laptop computer, or even a tablet, the experience would have been better. But for lower-tech mobile users, this website is practically *inaccessible*.

Megan tries to read a restaurant menu

Megan is partially sighted. She relies on a piece of software called a "screen reader" to read website content aloud to her in order to navigate the web. She's a confident user of the internet, being a digital native born in 2003, and the technology is second nature to her despite being partially sighted. It's a Friday afternoon and Megan wants to book a table at a restaurant for her and her partner that evening. A new French restaurant has opened in town and she decides to check out their website for offers, opening times, booking information and to read the menu. Her screen reader does its thing, listing out the pages on the website and eventually leading her to the restaurant's menu. But, as is so often the case, the menu is not a webpage; it is a *photograph* of the printed menu! The screen reader cannot interpret the text and so, Megan is unable to find out what is on the menu.

What is happening here?

It seems to be something of an industry custom that online restaurant menus are simply pictures of the physical menu or PDF downloads. This is probably because menus change quite often in terms of their content and format, and so maintaining this digitally can be a bit of a pain. However, if this menu was available as a web page with *real* text that can be read by a screen reader, Megan would not have been excluded. The menu is, in effect, *inaccessible*.

Did you know?

According to disability advocacy organisation Purple, businesses lose approximately £2bn/month by ignoring the needs of disabled people.[12]

Taking accessibility seriously

You might be thinking that these two examples hardly constitute a life or death situation. And you would be right. But the *ethos* of working with accessibility in mind is a good one, because people with varying needs experience challenges and exclusion on a daily basis. It all adds up. If you can make provisions to deliver a more accessible service, you should.

In the first example, Steven, despite actually having no disability, was presented with a poor mobile experience

---

[12] https://wearepurple.org.uk/the-purple-pound-infographic/

that impeded him from his goal of booking a GP appointment. In the second example, Megan was let down by a website that simply did not meet her needs. In the physical world businesses go to great lengths to ensure their services can be accessed, whether that is by providing wheelchair access to a building, easy read versions of important documents, or braille in public spaces. Many website owners would likely be mortified if they discovered just how inaccessible their online service actually is. Public sector websites in the UK are legally obligated to adhere to accessibility regulations[13], but no such regulation exists for charities or private business.

How to make your website accessible

When planning or developing a website, it is the perfect time to start thinking about accessibility. Unfortunately, there is no one size fits all approach to accessibility. The best way to ensure your work is accessible is to actually test it with your target audience. Here are a few tips to do this:

---

[13] http://www.legislation.gov.uk/uksi/2018/952/contents/made

- Ask your target readers what they would most want to get out of your online services

- Take some of your content and ask your readers to rewrite it in their own words

- Run a survey to gather feedback from your readers

- Conduct a test where you observe several readers using your website

- Have your readers describe your key content to you - do they see what you see?

By involving key website users you are likely to get more valuable information than by holding them at arms' length and guessing.

Alongside testing with real people, there are a number of technical solutions you should implement in order to meet accessibility guidelines. Here are some examples:

Avoid "read more" links

Links are what we use to get around the web. They are everywhere. They link pages together, and are typically denoted by an underline or some other way of making them stand out. Quite often, you'll see the words "learn more" or "read more" on the web. The problem with using words like this, is that without context they don't really mean anything. Read more... about what? Instead, use more intuitive link text, such as "read about our team" or "download our case study". It is possible to apply labels to nondescript links such as this, but it's often better to err on the side of caution and be as descriptive as is reasonable.

Ensure your website can be navigated with the keyboard

The reader should be able to hit the tab key on their keyboard to cycle through the links and content in an intuitive way. You can test this right now by going to any website and pressing the tab key. Note how each link becomes highlighted. Press the return key to activate this link. You've just navigated a website in much the same way as somebody who cannot use a mouse! As this happens automatically, you simply need to ensure that there is a sensible hierarchy to your content, with the most important links higher up the pecking order.

Describe your pictures

For people with low vision conditions, images can present issues on the web. Pictures and photographs are everywhere, and if they are crucial to understanding any accompanying text, blind or visually impaired people will miss out. To remedy this, be sure to add some "alternative text" to describe the image. Most content management systems such as WordPress enable you to do this, and social media networks now allow you to describe your image uploads as well. This is a positive move toward making our largest online social spaces more inclusive.

Limit usage of sliders/carousels

A feature found on many websites which you will undoubtedly have seen is the carousel, sometimes also called a slider. This is an area of the page that can be controlled by the user to move left/right between pieces of content. Its purpose is to make more use of limited space, and the idea behind it is pretty sound. However, I tend to urge people to stay away from them for a number of reasons. Firstly, they can be tricky to use as in many cases the navigation controls are not clear. This is compounded further if the carousel is set to automatically run, leaving the visitors confused as to what is going on. Secondly, it can be troublesome to deliver a good visitor experience on mobile and tablet devices, particularly if the carousel cannot be swiped by hand. Lastly, and most importantly, studies have shown time and again that hardly anybody actually engages with carousels.[14] So, carousels can be tricky to implement, tough to use, and most people do not use them anyway; and so my takeaway here is to avoid using them for any content that is of high importance. For secondary content, such as testimonials or partner logos, a carousel can provide an appropriate solution

---

[14] https://erikrunyon.com/2013/07/carousel-interaction-stats/

because this type of content is not typically interactive, nor does it contain vital information.

Only use hover menus if you have to

Hover menus are another common design idea that you will find all over the web. This refers to primary navigation menus that require the visitor hover their mouse pointer over in order to reach the content below. For example, imagine hovering your mouse over a menu link called "About Us" to reveal further options, such as "Our Team" and "Get In Touch". Once again, the thinking behind this is often to save space, or reduce clicks to get to key content. But for some users hover menus can present problems. For people with neurological conditions or motor problems making them prone to spasms, hover menus can be problematic, as you may imagine. In principle, there is nothing wrong with using hover menus if in fact the item being hovered is itself clickable. In the example above, the user should be able to click directly on "About Us" and be taken to a page with a submenu, *as well as* a hover menu being offered.

Check colour contrasts

What works for us might not work for others, so whenever you're using multiple colours be sure to check that any colour choices you make work well together. A quick way to do this would be to use the WebAIM

Contrast Checker
(https://webaim.org/resources/contrastchecker/).

Check your website structure

You might not be able to change the code that your website is built on, but you can check how well put together it is. Run your website through the WAVE Web Accessibility Tool (http://wave.webaim.org/) to see what problems need to be fixed. For errors and warnings outside of your ability to fix, be sure to check in with your website developer.

Shoot for the moon

There's a lot to take in here, and if you were mostly unaware of the importance of web accessibility before, you may feel this is something of a bombshell. If this is the case, I invite you not to worry, and to instead see this as an opportunity. The impact on workload in real terms is negligible; you simply need to follow a few best practices to work towards compliance. And the potential benefits of doing so will strengthen your digital offering all-round by introducing you to a wider audience and delivering a better online service. The underlying message here, if you take one thing away, is that you should become aware of the needs of others, and try your best to facilitate them.

Inclusion is good business

One of the reasons we see such poor accessibility on the web is because it can take time, which costs money, which is not viewed as a sound investment when compared to higher return activities such as marketing. But, according to the Web Accessibility Initiative (WAI) "Businesses that integrate accessibility are more likely to be innovative, inclusive enterprises that reach more people with positive brand messaging".[15] They go on to cite research that states the majority of Fortune 500 companies have developed and implemented diversity policies, many of which include people with disabilities in the definition of a diverse workforce. The statement by the WAI explores how accessibility can drive innovation, enhance your brand, extend market reach and minimise legal risk. Therefore, inclusive practice simply makes good business sense.

[15] https://w3c.github.io/wai-bcase/business-case/#fn:1

Chapter 10: LEVERAGING INTEGRATIONS

Want to know the trade secret to a successful website? Integrations. Essentially, an integration is the coming together of one or more pieces of software to share information. These parts, when joined, create something new and enable greater things than either part would on its own.

The technical method for bringing different pieces of software together is via something called an API (Application Programming Interface), and you've more than likely used APIs in the past as a consumer. Have you ever given an application access to your Facebook or Twitter account? This happens when you see a message that says "this application is requesting access to your newsfeed and contacts" or words to that effect, and then requires that you "authenticate". This authentication grants permission for the two applications to talk to each other. APIs can be found everywhere, and they're amazing. They let us developers do great things at low cost, leveraging the work of other tools and sharing data with ease.

What integrations might your website use?

The term integration implies a deep interoperability between software. However, in practice it can be very simple and light. Here are some examples of common integrations that you'll find all over the place:

- Newsletter signup forms that link into Mailchimp
- Usage analytics tracking scripts, such as Google Analytics
- Payment gateways, such as Stripe
- Social media feeds, such as Twitter and Facebook
- CRM forms, such as Salesforce (we'll cover CRM integration in more detail shortly)

Hopefully you have identified the pattern here: external tools are interfacing with your website via an API. The result, simply, is called a third-party integration. Having this tidbit of knowledge in your back pocket when communicating with developers and internal teams will give you the edge to make more sophisticated decisions about your charity's online presence. By linking into other systems, you get to create a robust website in a cost-effective way.

Quirkier uses for integrations

Integrations don't need to start and end with your website. There is a *service integration* company called If This, Then That (IFTTT.com) which enables disparate pieces of technology to talk to each other. A cursory glance at their website reveals some rather interesting and quirky uses for integrations, such as:

Turn on the porch lights when your Domino's pizza is being delivered (the two pieces of tech here are your internet-connected lights and your Domino's pizza app)

Switch off your Mac using your Amazon Alexa smart speaker

Round up purchases through Monzo banking to the nearest £1 and put the excess into a separate savings account.

If you're a little freaked out by these examples, don't worry. This is pretty cutting-edge stuff. That being said, we are moving quickly to a world of internet-connected devices (referred to as *The Internet of Things*) that will see a wide range of integrations between your physical devices, from your kettle to your alarm clock. *What a time to be alive!*

How deep is your integration?

A common question in website development is *how much integration is needed or wanted?* Your organisation might make use of lots of disparate tools, some of which may not need to talk to each other at all. You can get away with very few integrations if you don't mind a little inconvenience, such as logging into multiple pieces of software, or exporting data from one platform to another, but you might be willing to go a little deeper for extra fluidity and convenience. To illustrate this idea, let's look at three different levels of integration.

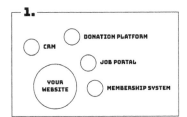

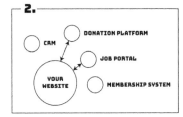

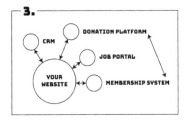

In the illustrations above I have demonstrated three varying depths of integration. In the first example, your website, CRM, donation platform, job portal and membership system all sit alongside one another but are not connected in any way. When somebody makes a donation, you have no visibility of how they found you or where they came from. In this case they might not have even visited your website; you just don't know. In the second example, which demonstrates a basic level of integration, you can see that the donation platform and the job portal are linked to your website. Your visitors can make a donation directly through your website, and your recruitment software can post jobs on your website that visitors can then apply to. In the third and final example, we see a more comprehensive system of integration, where not only your website is speaking to each piece of software that runs your organisation, but some of those tools also talk to each other. Imagine having a list of donors and a list of members, and needing to manually export the donations to mark against the appropriate records in your members system. Laborious, right? In this example, however, those two systems integrate with one another to share data, making your life easier and usually offering a smoother experience for the end user.

Integration depth is worth considering when scoping your project, but remember: you can always begin lightly and move toward a more robust solution over time.

The fallacy of the "all-in-one" solution

Despite it making sound business sense to leverage specialist platforms that dominate their industries (for example, why try to devise your own method for collecting and sending emails when Mailchimp exists?), every once in a while a company comes along that claims to *do everything*. One system to rule them all. Every competitor is left hopelessly redundant in the wake of these ingenious super-systems. It makes sense from a supplier's perspective because they feel they can hoover up lots more customers if they offer more things to more people. Heck, I'd be lying if I told you I hadn't been charmed by this route in the past.

However, if the "all-in-one" opportunity arises, exercise caution. The digital world is incredibly dynamic and fluid, and the ever-changing landscape of products, services and technologies means that any company claiming to have beaten the whole market with one, single product that doesn't rely on external integrations is likely being naively optimistic or very economical with the truth. The fact is that the plethora of tools and services on the web now enable organisations of all sizes to build great systems at low cost, using integrations. Yes, it can get messy, because each piece of software adds an additional moving part, but the benefits of doing so usually outweigh the negative, as you leverage industry-leading software to build out your best solution.

Suggesting the most appropriate API integrations for your project is very much within the remit of your website developer, so don't feel like you need to have all the answers here. However, having a clearer idea of what integrations are and how you can leverage them will help when defining project requirements, budgeting and communicating your ideas with others.

In the next chapter we'll be exploring one of the most useful integrations your organisation can invest in: a CRM database.

CHAPTER 11: INTEGRATING A CRM

A customer relationship manager (CRM) is vital for any organisation that manages more than a handful of contacts. Sometimes referred to simply as a database, your CRM will be the central place for storing and managing communications with both prospective supporters as well as existing stakeholders.

Charities, in particular, work with many individuals who require communicating with in different ways. You may segment donor groups by age or location so you can speak to them with more relevant messages. For example, if your charity works nationally, you may keep your donor records sorted by region. Alongside donor segmentation, you may want to communicate with completely different groups, such as volunteers or corporate partners.

These various lines of communication should be considered when setting up your website, because CRMs are typically integrated into your website using web forms. These forms may allow visitors to:

- Make donations
- Contact you
- Give feedback
- Register for newsletters
- Apply for jobs/volunteer roles

CRM integration means that you can systematically follow up these interactions in a sophisticated, and ideally automated way via a single channel. The forms on your website will link to your CRM and then that system will kick in to ensure you continue engaging with the person who submitted the form.

It's worth pointing out that a CRM project is a project in itself. It is not a trivial undertaking, and can require a good amount of planning and investment. My reason for featuring CRM in this book is because I believe it to be an important consideration for any organisation serious about its data management and comms.

The benefits of using a CRM

Leveraging a database helps to reduce your workload on tasks that are both simple and repetitive. For example, to become a volunteer at your organisation a person may download a Word document from your website, fill it out and then email it to you. You might then add their details to a spreadsheet for contacting later.

Think about how much time and resource this takes, and how needlessly complex it is. Imagine a better scenario, where the person completes a similar form on your website, and when submitted their details go directly into your CRM database. You get an email to notify you of this, and they get a "thank you" email in return. All done automatically, and without the need to maintain Word documents and spreadsheets. This how your CRM can benefit you; by reducing the drudge tasks that get in the way of important work.

Let me give you an example of a more sophisticated donor journey, this time using CRM rules to facilitate an automated donor journey:

1. You send out an email campaign to your supporters asking for their donations toward a particular appeal

2. A supporter receives the email and clicks a link that takes her to your appeal page

3. She reads the appeal page but does not make a donation

4. 48 hours later, she receives another email from you (sent automatically) asking again if she would like to donate.

Using CRM rules in this way we can determine what our supporters do and trigger actions accordingly. In this case, our supporter has clearly shown an interest in the appeal because she clicked the link and visited the website. She didn't make a donation on this occasion, but it makes sense to give her a friendly nudge later to ask again. This simple, automated process can do wonders for your conversion rate!

CRMs can also be configured to automatically unsubscribe those who never open your emails, which helps to keep your data clean and up to date. Automation and data veracity are just a couple of ways that a centralised database can support your comms strategy, so a CRM system is definitely worth considering if this is something your organisation is yet to explore.

Defining your stakeholder groups

Who are your stakeholders? For a non-profit organisation this would include trustees, staff and management, donors, fundraisers, volunteers, beneficiaries, service users and partners. It is worth spending the time to segment these groups so you have a clear idea of who they are and how you might communicate with them. Maintaining a relationship with donors is probably your key benefit to using a CRM, but you might also want to store other types of contacts in your database, such as corporate sponsors, even if you don't use the CRM to maintain a relationship with them. The real benefit of doing this is that these details are stored and maintained in one place. Dying are the days of keeping paper records, or emailing spreadsheets around your team to make changes. Your CRM will act as your "single source of truth"; the central point of reference for all your organisation's contacts.

Choosing a CRM

This, in my experience, is the most challenging of questions. Getting started is always the hardest part. The market is awash with CRM database solutions of all shapes and sizes, making it incredibly difficult to choose the right system for you. I'm going to assume that you're already sold on the idea of picking a CRM, so here are some questions to help you decide which one is right:

How many contacts will be in our database?

Some CRM products price themselves on *volume* rather than features, so write down an approximate number of contacts. Contacts can include donors, volunteers, staff; or any other stakeholder group that you need to keep in touch with. Your best guess here is fine, as you can scale later on.

How much support do we need?

CRM providers typically offer support packages to help you get set up and maintain a solid database. To answer this question, simply write down how confident you feel in running your CRM. If the answer is "not confident at all", this indicates that you may need a higher-tier level of support. In most cases, the lion's share of the support will be needed at the start, when setting up the database, with basic tech support offered ongoing.

How much automation do we want?

As outlined earlier, automation can be extremely powerful but a little tricky or costly to set up. In reality, most smaller organisations will only need the basics, but it is worth exploring what is possible and budgeting for it appropriately. If you're unsure at this stage, simply make a note to discuss these options with a CRM consultant or salesperson, who should be able to help you decide.

Will it integrate into our existing systems?

If you've read Chapter 10 on integrations you'll know how important interoperability is. When planning a CRM project it is worth thinking about how it will integrate with your existing software. In most cases, there shouldn't be any problems, but I've seen instances where an organisation is using some obscure piece of proprietary software that cannot be connected to anything. This makes the task of integration all the more challenging.

Integrating CRM forms on your website

Thinking about how you integrate your CRM with your website is helpful because it gives you a bigger-picture view of your comms strategy, as well as a deeper appreciation for how sections and pages may be linked together. Here are a few examples of pages on your website that you can place CRM forms to improve data management and comms:

Web page	Form	Why?
Blog article	Newsletter subscription form	If somebody is reading your news it is well worth asking them to subscribe for future updates.

Appeal/campaign	Donation form	If somebody is reading your appeal, their call to action should be to make a donation.
About your organisation	Contact form	If somebody is interested in learning more about you, they might be wanting to get in touch with you.

Can you think of any more?

Linking CRM to your content strategy

To understand how CRM and website content work together, consider the following example:

Imagine you are a charity that works in multiple parts of the country. You run appeals each month on your website, asking for donations to support the areas you work in. If somebody makes a donation to the Hull appeal, for example, it would then be prudent to only contact this donor about your impact in this specific area. Simple personalisation in this way provides a much more effective user experience and ensures your content strategy is tailored to the right people, at the right time. This is how sophisticated use of CRM and targeted, relevant content work beautifully together, and it can be used to foster far better relationships with donors than "send to all" emails and letters.

Using data to rehome more animals

In conjunction with IBM, the RSPCA developed a programmatic email campaign for people looking to rehome stray and abandoned animals. In practice, this meant a person looking to adopt would enter the details for their "perfect pet" on the RSPCA website and when this criteria is matched against new animals coming into the charity, the CRM would automatically notify that person.

This simple integration meant that more people were able to find pets that suited them, and led to more animals being rehomed.[16]

How to ensure CRM adoption

One of the challenges that advocates of CRM face is embedding its usage into the organisation, and I use the word "embed" with good reason. CRM is software, but it is not something you would simply tack-on to your

---

[16] https://www.youtube.com/watch?v=9zc3SDgda7g

charity and expect to work. Most CRM projects unfortunately fail and become self-fulfilling prophecies as they were approached with scepticism or non-commitment from the outset.

To integrate CRM effectively, you must understand that it is about mindset more than software. It maps how your organisation communicates, from the inside out. Here are a few tips for helping to encourage this mindset and embed CRM into your workflow:

Engage as many stakeholders as possible to hold discussions about CRM

The more involved people feel, the greater the chance of internal uptake. If your team feel a piece of software is being imposed on them, they'll simply be less inclined to use it. Consult with your colleagues to address their suggestions and concerns, and make them feel a part of the conversation.

Take a long-term view

Describe how a centralised database can add value by saving time and making you more efficient and ultimately, more effective. With a short-term investment you can yield greater gains later on. It makes total business sense.

Give responsibility to an individual to maintain the CRM

Much like the responsibility of looking after the website, CRM maintenance can be delegated to one person. I recommend doing this because it reduces the burden on the team at large, and proudly bestows the title of "database manager" onto one lucky individual. Every team has one, who's yours?

Bring on the legalspeak

The path to privacy compliance can be a tricky one to tread, and it is my opinion that the more elegant your comms systems, the harder it is to slip up here. CRM integration can simplify the way you hold and manage data, giving you a clearer view of your contacts and reducing any legal risks that may arise from poor data management. This alone should be a strong selling point.

I'm active in a number of non-profit online communities and the subject of CRM comes up time and again. There is confusion around which solution to choose, how much it might cost, and that is before we even come to deployment and adoption. It remains a challenging subject, but hopefully this chapter has given you some basic steps towards sourcing and integrating a database solution that works for you.

Chapter 12:
MANAGING YOUR PROJECT

Managing tech projects can be tough. There are always plenty of unknowns, and a healthy amount of trust is needed to work effectively with external suppliers. Larger projects, in particular, can become unwieldy and begin to spiral. For sure, good project management is a much sought-after skill.

In this chapter I'm going to tap into my experience of occupying various project roles, and discuss some ideas and techniques that I've seen used to keep things on track and running as smoothly as possible.

Working iteratively

In some cases, the urgency to produce a better online presence is strong. But sizeable projects can take some time to deliver. A sense of urgency coupled with what feels like a monumental task is a wonderful recipe for anxiety! Thankfully, there is a remedy for this.

The term "agile" in project management circles describes a process that encourages teams to make decisions quickly, but be absolutely open to having those decisions challenged later. The idea is to avoid analysis paralysis and just *get stuff done*. This is underpinned by an acceptance that your first attempt might not be perfect, and that you'll constantly gather feedback in order to iteratively improve. For perfectionists and control freaks, working like this can itself be a source of anxiety, but the benefits of allowing yourself to think in this way are multiple:

- Your task will feel less overwhelming because you can break it down into smaller chunks that can be delivered individually

- The need to create something perfect from day one evaporates as you accept nothing is ever perfect

- The idea of hard deadlines diminishes as you accept that everything is a work in progress

- Being open to changing what you've already done based on new data means that your work will be constantly improving

- It keeps things moving.

Time and again I have seen teams burned out and demoralised as their projects have dragged on for what feels like an eternity, labouring under an illusion that there is a *right time* to launch. However, we need quick wins to feel like we're making progress, and working iteratively using an agile approach enables this.

The MVP mindset

Within agile is this concept of an MVP - a Minimal Viable Product. An MVP is essentially the most basic version of something that meets a core need. The Windows application Notepad (or TextEdit, if you're a Mac user) is a solid example of an MVP. It allows you to type out some text, give it some basic formatting and then save it as a file on your computer's hard drive. Your vision might be Microsoft Word, with all its wonderful complexities and features, but imagine the challenge of developing that when all you really need in the first instance is the ability to create a text document. This is agile in action: creating the most basic version of something (Notepad) and iterating towards a more mature vision (Microsoft Word).

Putting agile into practice

The first step to applying agile to your projects is to decide on your *core requirements*, and nothing more. Note them down, and then develop your product or service to meet these needs. Once your work is out there in the wild, measure its value by asking for feedback and looking at any data available to you. Take your learnings, decide on what is needed and repeat the process all over again, and again, until your grand vision comes into focus. The beauty of agile is that once this vision begins to materialise, it will probably look nothing like it did when you first imagined it! That is largely the point: we're tempted to make all kinds of big decisions at the start of a project when ironically we know the least amount about it.

The essence of agile is to learn and improve by taking action frequently. Let us take a CRM project, for example. Your vision might be that of a fully-integrated system that manages relationships with thousands of your supporters using sophisticated automation techniques. But the problem with striving to reach this goal on day one means that your project will feel unwieldy and likely take a significant amount of time to implement. Instead, it would be preferable to launch your CRM sooner and build iteratively towards that vision. The flexibility that agile affords means that you can instantly remove the pressure to create something monolithic, and get something that works, in place sooner. In this case, it means completely forgetting about the clever stuff and focusing on the basics, like list segmentation and adding your contacts.

Hopefully you agree that launching early and seeing the benefits sooner makes far greater business sense than working away behind the scenes for several months on something that might not even provide the best solution when it finally launches.

Agile is certainly not the right approach for every project, or indeed every team, but for large and complicated projects it can help make them manageable and keep them moving.

Survival of the fittest

Another way to look at iterative working is to consider how it can ready your organisation for externalities that will impact your plans. This is bigger than your website, or your marketing strategy; it concerns the way you do business. Video rental company Blockbuster simply didn't respond to the changing business model of consumer entertainment, and was consequently squashed by streaming providers like Netflix. The market share of local taxi cab firms is being syphoned off by Uber because the industry at large has failed to spot the way in which smartphones have changed how we communicate. Taking a "survival of the fittest" view, where you are able to respond quickly to change, is a good practice in general.

Overcoming managerial challenges

I have been involved in hundreds of projects over my 15-year career in website development. Things can, and do, go wrong. Projects of any type can find themselves in crisis when:

- A key stakeholder exits, leaving a leadership void in their place
- Management and/or strategic objectives change
- New information supplants existing knowledge
- A conflict emerges between supplier and client, or internal team

The world needn't end if something like this happens; these can all be managed, so let's take a look at a few strategies for dealing with each scenario.

When leaders leave

I was once involved in a project that was being led by a marketing manager. A few weeks into the project I began to sense some tension within the company and, after following up a couple of unresponded emails, it turned out that the marketing manager had been "relieved of duty" and left the company. Content had been half-written, deadlines had been agreed, deposits had been paid. As it turns out, the manager herself was struggling against the weight of a chaotic organisation that didn't understand itself and was suddenly directing its fire my way.

My top tip for dealing with any such scenario is to ensure that a clear handover process happens, and that internal stakeholders and external suppliers be kept in the loop. In the end I was forced to end my relationship with this particular client, but better communication and a clear transfer of responsibility could have averted such a situation. As is so often the case, a simple line of communication between customer and supplier can help soften the toughest of situations.

When strategy changes

The introduction of a new decision-maker within your organisation can send shockwaves through any projects currently in development. It's not unusual for projects to be put on hold whilst a new CEO or marketing manager assesses the lay of the land. When this happens, in most cases little can be done other to communicate the situation to your stakeholders, both internal and if necessary, external. Are your fundraisers waiting on the website to begin a new campaign? Let them know the project is on ice.

To get ahead of any interruptions and changes that may come from above, it's best to emphasise the project's progress with any new decision-makers and if possible, give them the assurance that it can continue with only their minimal involvement needed (unless, of course, this is not the case). This builds the case for *letting you get on with it* with minimal disruption. Conversely, there may actually be value in stopping to take stock at this point. If this happens, read on.

Handling new information

Sometimes, we get halfway through a project and realise that something about what we're doing is wrong. Perhaps we misjudged something, or new data has come to light that means we must reassess our current position. When this happens we have two choices: we stop, reflect and reconfigure our path accordingly, or we push ahead, not wanting to feel like our time so far has been wasted.

I've found in many cases the instinct is to push on with the original plan. But the problem with this approach is that you end up simply delaying the inevitable. Nothing can stand in the way of change, and when the pressure mounts, burying your head in the sand can be the worst response. In the end, you need to respond to that pressure.

Let us imagine that your team has spent weeks planning your website. The sitemap has been agreed, content has been written, and design work is underway. In order to involve your stakeholders, you make all the right moves by inviting early feedback from a pool of your fundraisers. This exercise proves somewhat unpalatable, however, as their feedback indicates some fundamental holes in your earlier planning. In an ideal scenario, you would have sought their feedback earlier, but now you have their thoughts, what do you do? It would be tempting to press on. You've done your research, *you know best*. But a failure to acknowledge the concerns of your stakeholders in this way will only result in their dismay down the line!

In order to integrate new ideas midway through a project, it helps to work in an iterative fashion, as discussed earlier. If you can't respond to change quickly, the cost of responding later can be heavy, so it is a good idea to be open to constant feedback as your project develops.

Dealing with a disagreement with your supplier

Conflict can arise between customer and supplier. Thankfully this happens rarely, but it does happen. If you're unhappy with your supplier the best way to deal with the situation is to communicate clearly and assertively, as early as possible. Do not let ill feelings fester. Clarity is key here - when dealing with technical projects that often carry a learning curve, it can feel like you're being left in the dark at times. This won't be an intentional move on your suppliers part, and it's important to remember that we all have varying communication styles. Understand this, but if the situation shows no sign of resolution, check the terms of your contract to see what rights you have and how the project might be ended.

Dealing with feedback

So far, a continuing theme in this book has been advocating the process of working in collaboration with others. Engaging others is not only a great way to build a better product - it can also help smooth the transition from old to new when your work finds its way out into the world. But this alone won't protect you from the might of other people's opinions, so if your role is to manage the project to a successful launch, let's look at a few strategies for dealing with this.

Ask for feedback

Making people feel like their voice is being heard is important in business but I would argue it's even more vital in the non-profit sector. You obviously cannot involve every individual stakeholder in the development process, but you can reach out and ask for their thoughts later on. Be sure to contact your existing stakeholders and ask for their input. Do this in the form of an online survey or telephone conversation, and try to resist the urge to welcome freeform feedback over email as this will get unwieldy.

Leverage social media

Monitoring social media, particularly in the first few weeks of launching your website, is crucial. The relative anonymity that Twitter affords means that people feel safe to air their uncensored thoughts about you and your work. Most of your feedback will be positive, but be sure to grasp the negative early and respond constructively. Don't feed the trolls, but it's prudent not to ignore negative feedback either, as this can encourage the voices to become louder.

Examine your analytics

Analytics data that tells you how engaged your visitors are provides a form of "non-verbal" feedback. This can give you clues on how well your new website is being received. We cover this in more detail in Chapter 14.

Provide a beta website

If you can, make your new website available to the public a few weeks before its official launch. Use this as an opportunity to talk about your plans and build some momentum behind your project. This can prepare your audience for the changes ahead as well as deliver some interesting pre-launch feedback.

Responding to feedback

Thanking people for their feedback is always the first step, but how do you go about integrating their thoughts into any future work? My advice is to collate their responses and look for common themes. Perhaps you've identified that several people struggled to find a particular resource, or maybe the navigation fails to work on a particular device or web browser. By being open to hearing the experiences of others you'll no doubt become aware of your own blind spots during development. If a common problem is identified, take the time to let people know you're working on it. This could be in the form of a blog post, social media message or email notification.

Be aware also, that not all feedback is useful. Some suggestions can be politely dismissed, but when it comes to integrating the valuable comments I advise you implement some of the ideas discussed earlier. This is where working iteratively can help manage your feedback: simply note down the most important comments, such as errors on the website, and resolve to tackle these first.

My closing piece of advice concerning feedback of any kind is to ensure you actually engage in a process to respond to it. Don't bury your head in the sand and ignore it, because it will eventually catch up with you, as these things tend to do. Listen, respond and improve.

As I outlined at the beginning of this chapter: project management is tough! The role of the PM is all-encompassing and it doesn't stop at project launch. Good PMs involve relevant stakeholders, make their team feel valued and are open to having past decisions challenged. This requires letting your guard down and trusting those around you, and if you work in this way, your website project is far more likely to run smoothly.

Chapter 13:
GENERATING INCOME ONLINE

One of the primary goals of the charity website is to generate income from new and existing supporters. It's often very tempting to whack a PayPal button at the top of the page and hope for a wave of generous donations, but in all likelihood your website will need to work a little harder than this to earn support.

You achieve this by going through the processes outlined in this book: understanding your visitors by creating personas, producing content that engages your readers and by developing relationships elsewhere online in order to build your brand. Only when you've done the work will you see the pay-off. Now let's take a look at some of the ways in which you can multiply your income through your website:

Processing donations

You'll be hard-pressed to find a non-profit website that doesn't let you make a donation online, so I thought it made sense to tackle this most obvious revenue opportunity first. There are, as is so often the case, plenty of things to consider here:

- Do you want donors to claim Gift Aid (and do you have the back office facilities to deal with this)?

- Do you want donors to set up recurring monthly payments?

- Do you mind if the payment process takes donors off-site to a third-party provider?

- Do you want to let supporters set up their own fundraising pages?

- Do you want to allow anonymous donations?

- Is your website secure in order to handle financial transactions?

Most donation systems, whether integrated or third-party, will provide the basics. But it's important to try to answer these questions early on in the process so that you can make resources available in order to carry out these decisions well. Sometimes, your expectations don't align with that of your website developer or wider team, so be very clear from the outset exactly what sort of features your online donation mechanism needs to have.

Integrated vs off-site donation function

For the avoidance of confusion, by integrated donation I mean a donation process that does not ship the donor off to another website, such as JustGiving. There are a number of key benefits to keeping donors on your website:

- The donation can be easily tracked by your analytics software
- Data can be automatically captured by your CRM database
- Your thank you page can be customised

  However, utilising a third-party system such as JustGiving to process donations also carries its benefits:

- It can be quicker and cheaper (in the short term) than an integrated system
- Donors know and trust JustGiving

Weigh up these options with your team, and know that nothing is set in stone. A third-party solution could be a temporary measure, and an integrated system could be enhanced over time.

In reality, a clever combination of on-site and off-site fundraising is the most savvy approach for your organisation as a whole. Whilst you might run campaigns on your own website, you may also run Facebook fundraising appeals at the same time. This means you'll reach supporters *where they are*, whether that's on your website or social media channels.

Other ways to generate revenue

Aside from processing donations, many charities are now seeking to become more self-sufficient by selling products or services. These can be physical products such as branded mugs and t-shirts, as well as digital products such as training materials, memberships and event tickets. These additions have the potential to add immense value to your website and ultimately your organisation as a whole, enabling you to deliver a greater impact on the communities you serve.

There are now many options for selecting an e-commerce solution, and integrations are your friends here. Beware the "all-in-one solution" (see Chapter 10). Seek systems that plug into others and work well together. For example, if a website visitor purchases a membership from you, along with processing their payment you may also want their details to go into a CRM system so that you can follow up your relationship with them. This might require two pieces of software that integrate with one another via an API (see Chapter 10). It sounds scary, but as I have hopefully expressed, APIs have made delivering fantastic web services easier and cheaper over the years.

Depending on the sort of products you are wanting to sell, different systems are available to you. Let's take a look at some examples.

Ticket sales

If your charity runs events frequently and the revenue is integral to your income, an integrated system would be recommended because it will help to maximise your profit on sales. If selling tickets is not especially important to you and it isn't something you do often, a third-party provider such as Eventbrite.com might be more suitable to handle the transaction. The benefit of using Eventbrite is that it is a robust system for selling tickets with an existing audience ready to find your events. The downside is that they charge fees that either your attendees or you need to foot the bill for, and visitors are clearly buying from a company external to your own. With an integrated solution, you control everything; the look and feel, and the fees. Once again, balance the options available to you to make the best decision, and know that you can change your mind later.

Physical products

If your organisation creates its own physical products such as t-shirts, you'll want a simple e-commerce store from which to let people buy them. If this is an area you're just starting out in, I strongly recommend using whichever platform makes this easiest for you. Don't worry about deep integration into your website, or white-labelling the brand. Don't concern yourself with fees and making a big profit. The e-commerce market is huge, and you could drive yourself up the wall trying to find the *perfect solution.* I repeat: don't try to become Richard Branson if you're new to the e-commerce game; just focus on getting something that *works*.

If you're using WordPress, there are a number of plugins available. The most commonly used is WooCommerce, which is a suite of plugins that enables you to pull together the right solution for your needs. Alternatively if you'd like to set something up really quickly, take a look at Shopify.

Memberships

Memberships are an increasingly popular method for generating recurring revenue within the third sector. This is due to a number of factors: a squeeze on funding has forced charities to look elsewhere for income, the technology is now available to create membership websites more easily, and charities realise they can do this online with more sophistication than a downloadable payment form. Memberships are fantastic because they not only generate cash, they enable you to build a community, and one that you can easily engage with.

There are a number of options for delivering a membership solution either via your website or as a standalone system. It really depends on what features you need. For example:

- How many members do you have? How many members do you *expect* to have?

- Are they local, national or international?

- Do you want members to log in on your website to find exclusive content?

- Should members pay through your website, or does it matter if they are directed elsewhere?

- Do you want a single system to communicate with members, or are you happy to connect to other pieces of software via an integration?

- What internal resource, such as moderators, might be needed?

Sometimes, and much like when scoping out CRM requirements, it can make sense to look at a membership system as a separate project. This approach means that you could effectively plug the system in at a later date in order to speed up the development time of your website project.

Working towards sustainability

There is mixed data on the status of charitable giving in the UK and the US. Whether your particular organisation stands to see its income rise or fall depends on a number of factors. There are multiple ways to look at the various data samples available, and whilst I believe it is important to do so, my general position is that charities should be protecting themselves by building additional income streams as outlined in this chapter. Grant funding is becoming ever more precarious, and new charities are being created all the time. The need to differentiate and stand out among the competition will become even more important, and as technology allows non-profits to do greater things online, the need for income diversification will become ever more vital.

Charitable giving is built around the idea of emotional currency, but non-profits shouldn't rely solely on this for their income and would do well to look at other ways in which they can add value to the communities they serve. If this chapter has inspired you to think about how you might achieve that, read on as we discover how to measure your return on this investment.

CHAPTER 14: MEASURING YOUR ROI

Every website design project will have different versions of what success looks like. But remember that you're not doing this (just) for fun, and that you're going to want to see a return for your efforts. This will likely be seen as an uptick in donations, more subscribers to your mailing list, more corporate partners; the list goes on. In this chapter I'm going to explain how you can measure your Key Performance Indicators (KPIs) with web analytics, as well as track your actual goals using the AIDA marketing model (don't worry, it's fairly simple!).

Using web analytics effectively

A new website might not deliver results immediately, but you can immediately see what impact your redesign is having by looking at your website analytics. Here are the KPIs to look out for - and they're especially powerful when compared against the same metrics from your old website.

How long do people spend on your website?

Take a look at your "average time on site" or "average session duration" number. How high is it? Is it higher than it was the month before you launched your new website? Lower? There is little point in me telling you what this number *should* be, because it can vary massively. If this number is low, it could be because you don't have much content, or because your content is not engaging enough for your readers to fully consume it. If you feel this number is too low, think about how you can improve your content generally to make it clearer, more accessible or more interesting. With every piece of content you write, think "who would read this and why?"

How many pages do people visit?

Like "average time on site", the number of pages that people visit on your website can be taken as an indicator of how interested they are in your content. However, it's important not to feel too downhearted if this number is low; it may be the case that you are actually serving your visitor's needs well. Consider this - a visitor, searching Google for "postnatal depression support in Manchester" - enters your website on a page that provides *all* the information they need. At this point, they might email or telephone you, then leave the website. In this case the visitor will have viewed only the one page, but the visit would have been a success.

If you want *more* engagement however, think about how you can pepper your content with links to related pages, enticing the reader to go elsewhere on the website. Speaking very generally, if the average number of pages viewed per visit is very low, it is an indication that your content could be working harder.

What's your bounce rate?

Your bounce rate is established by how often visitors leave on the same page they entered, without visiting any other pages in between. Contrary to popular misunderstanding, the visitor does not "bounce" away immediately; they could very well spend 10 minutes on the page; but if they leave without looking at anything else, this is considered a bounce. Averaging out this activity across all visitors produces an average "bounce rate".

Much like the average number of pages viewed, a high bounce rate is not necessarily an indicator of failure, but when taken alongside a low average time on site and a low average pages viewed, it builds a picture that suggests the overall experience you're offering visitors could be improved.

Insider tip: don't *only* use Google Analytics

When it comes to web analytics, Google is not the only player in town. GA provides raw data about your traffic but sometimes it's useful to look at other factors. Here is the software that I use:

Hotjar.com is an analytics tool that anonymously records visitors as they browse your website. This offers a more qualitative insight into the mind of each user and helps catch common problems that enable you to make minor improvements to your website.

Leadfeeder.com is a piece of software that attempts to tell you which organisation your visitor is from. This can be useful if you want to proactively target an organisation for their support, if you've seen that they have initially shown an interest in your website.

These different ways of looking at your web traffic can help to unlock potential new ways to create content and engage with your visitors.

Using the AIDA model

Now that we've taken a brief look at website analytics, I feel it is important to expand on how you can use this data to look more deeply into your marketing efforts.

If you're investing time and money into your website, it needs to add value to your organisation. And that value must be measurable. The best way to determine this value is to set goals and measure your progress toward achieving them.

There is an elegant method that I like to use to measure my progress toward some goal. The AIDA model is a well-established technique used by marketing professionals to describe the steps taken through, typically, a sales process. It goes like this:

AIDA: Awareness > Interest > Desire > Action

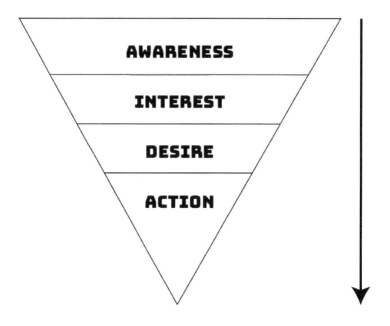

The AIDA model can be thought of as a funnel, carrying your prospective supporters down to finally take some desired action.

Let's take a look at each step in more detail.

Awareness

It doesn't matter whether you are seeking to recruit volunteers, reach service users or get new donors; nothing happens if nobody is aware of you. The greatest website in the world is a pointless investment if nobody sees it. So how might you measure the level of awareness of your organisation in light of a new website or marketing strategy? Here are some things you can look at to track awareness:

- Website traffic - are more people coming to your website thanks to your marketing?
- Social media engagement - are you getting more shares and comments?

These are indicators of how many people are *aware* of your organisation and your services.

Interest

Once somebody becomes aware of your organisation, the next step is to gain their interest. You do this by making sure that your website content is engaging and relevant, but how do you know if this is the case? Here are some metrics to track *interest* in your services:

- Average number of pages viewed per visit - are people intrigued enough to click around your website?
- How long do people spend on your website?
- How many visitors return to read your blog?

We discussed some of these metrics in the previous section but it is worth reiterating here in the context of the AIDA model.

Desire

So, you have a high number of returning visitors and people are engaging with your content. Well done! Most websites fail to achieve this. Now your task is to engage these people sufficiently as to provoke a *desire* to work with you in some way. You do this by fostering some emotional response in your reader. This is where the waters can muddy in regards to marketing techniques, so tread carefully. We don't want to lie or manipulate, but it's not uncommon for non-profits to use emotive wording and imagery to encourage support. These activities create a sense of urgency and conjure an emotional response in your reader to *do something*. Here's how you might get a view on how this is working for you using analytics:

- Drop-offs - do would-be donors begin the process but stop halfway through?

- Repeat page views - do specific appeals garner more repeat interest than others?

- Which content is being most widely shared?

- Are your videos watched until the end?

This data points to which content is creating the most emotional response. Understand it, and expand on the stuff that's working.

Action

Actions - or goals - are what it's all about. Everything you've done so far comes down to this. You've brought somebody from a position of ignorance through the AIDA funnel and prompted them to support you in some way. You can track actions by looking at enquiries, donations, volunteer applications or whatever is appropriate to your organisation.

To recap, let's look at a fictional example:

Anne is a part-time mature student who has found herself one day a week free and she wants to give her time to the local community. But how? She knows that homelessness is a big problem in her city and so jumps onto Google and searches "volunteer at homeless charity". Eventually, she is led to your website. Because you have spent time producing content that answers her questions ("how much time do I need to give?", "in which areas would I need to work?", "would I be given training?"), piqued her desire to help ("there are approximately 70 people sleeping rough in your city tonight") and provided clear calls to action ("fill out this short volunteering form to get started"), Anne has gone from not knowing you exist to sending a volunteer application. You have successfully led her through your AIDA funnel to action!

Measuring your true ROI can be tricky, and in my experience not enough of us give it due attention. Using the methods discussed in this chapter should help you to establish the right metrics to track, and give you a process for developing your marketing funnels. Once you begin to understand which of your activities produce the best outcomes, you can be much more savvy with the way you spend your time and money, and focus on the most rewarding aspects of your work.

"Half the money I spend on advertising is wasted; the trouble is I don't know which half."

This quote, attributed to marketing pioneer John Wanamaker 150 years ago is timeless. Even with the best intent, it can seem impossible to measure your marketing results. So where do you begin? Start small and examine the traffic carefully to establish any connecting threads and trends that produce the "best" traffic (whatever that might look like to you). Then do more of it.

Chapter 15:
LEARNING FROM OTHERS

Whilst writing this book I conducted a number of interviews with those working for and in the non-profit sector in a digital capacity. I explore their work here in the form of case studies, giving you insights into their ways of working and hopefully inspiring you to integrate some of their ideas into your own projects.

These stories are outlined below, and you can watch the video interviews on here: thedigitalcharity.co.uk/interviews.

Building online communities - Carley Centen

Carley works for a non-profit organisation that raises awareness of Child Sexual Exploitation (CSE) and provides support for those affected by it. The charity wanted to explore ways in which the digital medium may be leveraged to facilitate peer support, and settled on the provision of a private online forum to enable parents to connect in a secure online space. Carley was instrumental in the delivery of this project and was happy to tell me a little more about it.

Creating a sense of security

CSE is a sensitive topic, and so security and service user safety was of paramount concern to the project. To make sure that the charity deployed the forum in a suitable way, Carley conducted research and interviews with service users. High on the conversational agenda was anonymity, and the challenge of creating a space that enabled anonymous peer interaction balanced with user safeguarding. Key to this process was also learning by example: how had other charities approached this challenge?

Choosing the right platform

The market for social platforms is vast, and so choosing the right solution for your particular needs can be tricky. For Carley, privacy was paramount. Not just the process for registering and using the platform, but customisation and the ability to control the environment. A concern from the board was that if any sensitive content leaked it could result in not just a PR disaster for the charity, but could also damage ongoing court cases and have a devastating impact on the lives of those affected. Therefore, the ability to completely control the community was necessary. This meant using a WordPress-driven forum integration, where configuration and data was all kept in-house, rather than utilising some third-party solution where this was not the case (or was not guaranteed to be the case in future).

Gathering and integrating feedback

The forum project was initially a pilot that ultimately became a new service delivery stream. But as with any business development project the benefits must outweigh the cost. In this case, the key metrics for success were around emotional connection and the feeling of being less isolated. In order to achieve this, the community needed to firstly feel that they had a stake in its existence. One of the features that Carley had established early on in the process was the need to assign specific "roles" to users of the forum to promote shared ownership. The organisation would run "moderator of the week", which allowed members a moderating role within the forum. The numbers were not high (somewhere in the region of 40-50 people) so this approach was both practical and effective.

How can small charities develop their own online communities?

A continuing theme of this project, and one that threads through to the very end of this case study, is one of user engagement. As service providers we typically see ourselves as just that: providers of a service. But Carley stresses the need to see past the idea of "build it and they will come". If you involve stakeholders at an early stage and keep them engaged throughout the process, the chances of your endeavour succeeding (whatever it is) improves greatly. As the developer of a community, it was Carley's role to act chiefly as a facilitator. It was her job to establish a clear destination, and then enable the beneficiaries of that goal to walk her on that journey.

Using personas to understand your stakeholders
- Vikram Singh

Vikram is the senior UX (user experience) designer at Lightful, a SaaS (software as a service) product designed to help charities maximise their potential using social media. I covered persona development in Chapter 8 but for this case study I wanted to speak with Vikram, who has significant experience in this area, in order to share some deeper insights on how you can develop and use personas in your own organisation.

What are personas?

The persona idea was conceived by software developer Alan Cooper in the 1990s[17] as a way to put the end user at the heart of decision-making. Until this time, design decisions were typically made by the engineers building the product, based largely on their own interpretations. This goes some way to explaining why a lot of software (and hardware) seems unfathomable to the ordinary person. Cooper's approach was to invert this paradigm

---

[17] https://www.cooper.com/journal/2008/05/the_origin_of_personas

and encourage developers to start responding directly to the questions and needs of their users. To do this, developers needed to begin engaging their users in ways they had not previously, through the medium of interviews and other forms of research. From this data, teams would spot trends in their user base and begin to formulate fictional characters, called personas. These personas typically have names and pictures, and describe one or two core concerns.

In the case of Lightful, Vikram and his team engaged users to find out more about what they wanted from the product. Common themes included "what makes a good social media post?" and "how can we increase our followers?" This forces the team to continually address these needs in everything they do. Instead of seeing the software as a "tool that posts content to social media", Lightful can pitch itself as a tool for improving social media engagement or saving time; thus answering the real needs of their customers.

Why use personas?

Core to the idea of using personas, Vikram says that the process helps to develop empathy for the end user. By giving them names and faces, personas add a level of clarity to the way we think about our users in ways we might easily miss. If you have a persona called Susan, who is a busy single mother living in an area with poor infrastructure, you can connect with the idea of how best to serve her than if she were a faceless, nameless service user. In practical terms, this means that when you're thinking up a new appeal, or changing the way you deliver a service, your team can ask in earnest: "how would Susan feel about this?"

This approach enables you to see your stakeholders in a more human way.

Start with research, not guesswork

User research is at the heart of persona creation, and all personas should be based on the research you conduct. Vikram advises that personas should never simply be "made up". This is because personas are designed to shed light on how users *feel*, and even the most empathetic of us can't know everything. Furthermore, research leads to more evidence-based decision-making on your part, so whilst persona design might at first feel a little woolly at first, it can result in a highly valuable asset for your organisation.

Be open to having your assumptions challenged

The exercise of creating personas is as much about the process as it is the outcome. We all have preconceived ideas about who our target users are, and these ideas may even prove to be somewhat accurate, but by speaking with your users you can find out so much more.

Vikram offers an example from Lightful, whose users are charitable organisations. The user of the software must allow the platform access to their social media accounts in order to create and post content, but research suggested that many potential customers were put off by this for fear of what it may entail. Would security be compromised? The tech-savvy team at Lightful know that in most instances, giving third-party software access to your social accounts is not a concern. But some of their customers didn't, and it prevented them from using the platform. Vikram's team, through user research and persona development, identified this blind spot in their own thinking and used this data to update their marketing messages as well as the user journey within the software application. By directly addressing a clear barrier, the team were able to handle any concern from would-be customers.

How small charities can develop and use personas

Small charities are renowned for having a deficit of time, resource or money (and sometimes all three). Fortunately, from a financial perspective at least, Vikram makes it clear that creating personas is an investment of time, *not* money. You may incur sundry expenses when interviewing stakeholders, but the real investment is in conducting the up-front research in order to effectively carry out your persona work. What this looks like will depend on your personal approach, but it could involve face to face interviews with service users, telephone conversations or questionnaires. You would then consolidate your research notes into themes using something called "affinity mapping". This sounds complex, but in reality it is simply a case of visually organising your thoughts coherently and in such a way that your team can understand and agree. This is crucial because personas will be ignored if the team do not feel they add value. Once personas have been created, Vikram suggests keeping them at the forefront of the team's thinking by ensuring they are always visible. "Put them up on the wall, bring them into meetings and ensure you have an agenda item to discuss them" is his advice, and this will ensure that they don't get hidden away in a drawer, never to see the light of day again.

Another important aspect of working with personas is the need to review and update them from time to time. Are they still fit for purpose or do they need to be tweaked? How accurate were they, and what has been learned? Doing this enables new knowledge to be fed back into your organisation which can be used to constantly serve your stakeholders in the best possible way.

If you want to grow your supporters and impress your funders, creating personas based on what they expect of you is a wonderful way to get ahead.

Developing new services using co-creation principles
- Mandy Barker

Mandy heads up Sail, a creative agency that designs for real-world impact. I was interested in speaking with Mandy after learning of the work her team had done with Newcastle Carers, an organisation that supports people with caring responsibilities.

Sail was commissioned to help raise awareness of the caring responsibilities of people aged 18-24 in Newcastle via a creative campaign. Many young people with caring duties do not identify as carers, and so the ultimate objective of the campaign was to reach this audience to make them aware that support is available to them. In order to effectively connect with an audience, the team understood that engaging existing stakeholders to learn from them can be a valuable approach. The tangible outcome from this project was a billboard campaign that was effectively co-designed with the young adult carers who work with Newcastle Carers. This case study outlines the journey that Sail, Newcastle Carers and their young service users embarked upon.

Working with young adult carers

To start the project, Sail ran a number of workshops with the young people who work with Newcastle Carers.

The key objective of these sessions was to build a relationship with these young carers so that trust could be established, and to create an environment where mutual learning can take place. Mandy's team began by introducing the carers to the principles of effective design, discussing the merits of photography, illustration and typography. This was to cultivate an awareness of the marketing messages that we all receive on a daily basis, and to help the participants identify and understand what makes an effective piece of advertising. Armed with this knowledge, the group would talk about their design preferences; what spoke to them, and even put together printed collages to experiment with visual direction. The idea was to create a sense of ownership of the work, empowering the carers to *lead* this process whilst Sail opted for a more facilitating role.

Mandy's team recognised that this format appeals to some people more than others, and so to ensure inclusivity they ran both group and individual activities. The pay-off in doing this was not just that everybody's voice was heard, but that every individual was motivated and engaged throughout.

The benefits of collaborative design

Most creative design projects are delivered from the top down. Ideas are pitched, a team is recruited, money changes hands and a campaign is delivered. This may be the commercially accepted way in which design work is done, but Mandy thinks that Sail's co-design approach is more progressive and yields better results. She refers to it as "radical", and I would be inclined to agree. The process the team followed was highly effective not because of the creative outputs but *because* of the process. Its collaborative nature energised all stakeholder groups, built confidence and created a momentum within the organisation that simply would have been absent using a more traditional delivery method.

How would a charity engage in co-design?

Mandy's key piece of advice is to be comfortable with the unexpected. This can be extremely difficult when working within the confines of budgets and deadlines, but creativity always needs some breathing space to flourish. In this case, creativity was brought to the table not just from the aspect of delivery, but from the process followed. Mandy's team went into it with no creative concepts, but with a simple trust that engaging those who are already invested would produce the best solution.

For me, the takeaway from this case study is one of moving towards a facilitatory position where your stakeholders take centre stage in order to learn from them, rather than attempting to prescribe the outcome from the sidelines.

Developing a content strategy - Emmelie Brownlee

Emmelie is the digital comms manager at Bioregional, a sustainability charity that works with businesses and communities across the world to create happier, healthier lives for everyone within the limits of our planet. In 2018, the organisation had the opportunity to redesign their website, and Emmelie recognised that developing compelling content was key to the success of any future digital work the organisation does. Having covered the importance of thoughtful content extensively in this book, I'm happy to share Emmelie's story with you.

Why revisit content when building a new website?

It is often the case that website content lacks focus, especially with the passing of time, and the previous Bioregional website was no exception to this rule. The team recognised that a lot of content had accumulated over the years, and though much of it had value, it was not held within any coherent structure and lacked an underlying purpose. The motivation for auditing and repairing the content during website redesign was to provide real value to readers and funnel them toward some kind of action. In this case, generating leads by encouraging people to get in touch was one of the main goals that Emmelie's team set out to achieve. When building a new website it is tempting to simply design around existing content, hoping for the best; when in fact the real need is to revisit the content from its core.

Knowing your audience

The website design process is a great opportunity to assess existing content because it enables you to reacquaint yourself with your key audiences. At Bioregional, the team went through this process with their web development company to understand who would be engaging with their content and how to answer their needs. Emmelie then audited all content based on these described audiences in order to modify it or delete it, and to uncover any gaps within the overall content strategy. An additional benefit of producing content based on clear user needs is that specific search terms can be discovered and implemented, boosting the SEO value of the website as a whole and ensuring the right content is provided at the right times.

Keeping everybody happy

Those close to an organisation, and long-serving members of staff, tend to have a deep connection with the way the organisation presents itself to the world. This is entirely understandable, and no organisation could succeed without a certain level of emotional buy-in from at least a small percentage of its staff. The flip side of this truth is that it can present challenges when it comes to redesigning how the charity communicates, because everybody wants to have their say. To deal with this challenge, Bioregional, working with their web development team made sure to bring internal stakeholders along on the journey. In practice, this meant defining key goals for the content and the website itself, and therefore empowering the team to coalesce around a shared vision. It makes it significantly more difficult to argue over the value of a piece of content if its very existence is determined by an agreed framework.

To further ease the transition from old to new, the team decided to immortalise older, less relevant content in the form of heritage pieces and archived case studies. This is a wonderful solution to a common problem that organisations of all sizes face when auditing their content.

Ensuring that content keeps on giving

Another common situation that businesses and charities find themselves in once a set of content has been produced, is continuing to get value out of it and building on it as part of an ongoing strategy. It's easy to think that these things are "done" once they're done. But good marketers know that this work is never done, and any successful content strategy needs to think about the future. For Emmelie's team this meant developing a culture of appreciation for content more generally, and a recognition that good content is the cornerstone of any successful comms strategy. They achieved this, in part, during the website redesign process itself but also by running internal seminars to continue to involve stakeholders with the comms decisions moving forward. On a more practical level, they developed template documents so that specific types of content (i.e. case studies) can be produced within a clear structure. This not only encourages activity moving forward, it promotes a level of consistency and quality for the work being produced.

The results of this work speaks for itself, as the new Bioregional website sets out a clear statement of intent from the moment you see it. Emmelie and her team demonstrate what can be achieved when every piece of content is considered, scrutinised and forced to answer the question "what purpose does this serve?"

When conducting these interviews, what struck me most was how much dedication was given to each project. When individuals and teams come together to focus on a shared goal, amazing things can happen. From Carley's forum project that provided a space for service users to connect, to Mandy's radical approach to co-production; it is clear that including stakeholders in the process can be very fruitful. Taking the time to investigate the needs of your audience and produce content and services especially for them, as demonstrated in Vikram and Emmelie's projects, adds further credence to the idea of user-centred design.

What can you take away from this? Which ideas covered here can be applied to your organisation? Sit down with your team and discuss ways in which you can tune up your marketing, content production and service delivery to strengthen your charity's offering.

Chapter 16:
STAYING ACTIVE

People talk of business plans as "living documents", and in a way your website is a manifestation of this same idea. It is never finished, and it responds to the changing environment around it. It must be kept alive. Take care of your website, and it will take care of you. Here are a few simple, actionable things you can to do to ensure your website does not stagnate post-launch.

Make it somebody's responsibility

As we've discovered, the website development process is creative and messy and relies on the input of various stakeholder groups. But once the fun is over, it makes sense to delegate key responsibility for the website to one person. Why?

- This person will be solely accountable
- Any changes or updates will be fed through a single point of contact
- It prevents too many hands from grasping the steering wheel and driving in all myriad of directions.

In short, if maintaining the website is everybody's problem then nobody will actually take ownership and all your hard work will be for nothing. By delegating core responsibility to just one person, that person will treat the website with special consideration. Yes, humans are weird.

Use social media

Especially if you choose to include social media feeds on your website, you're going to want to keep these fresh. Not only does it show visitors that you are active, if you engage with your community on social media it will help to bring in a steady stream of relevant traffic. Don't neglect your social channels and try to update them with some frequency. Don't put content out there for the sake of it, but do try to share some interesting updates at least a couple of times a week.

Perform content audits

Remember all that content you produced during the website build project? A lot of it will go out of date. Strategic objectives change, contact details change, trustees and staff come and go and you need to have a plan in place to make sure the website reflects this. Making changes as and when needed is the best way to keep on top of it, but I recognise that it might not be your number one priority. Therefore, make a note to sit down every 6-8 weeks to spend an hour auditing your website content. Ask yourself what needs to be updated or added, and what can be deleted. Keeping on top of this is important in order to prevent the overall website experience degrading over time.

Write on your blog

How many times have you visited a company's blog to find they last posted 18 months ago? It's not a good look. I am absolutely guilty of letting this slip myself. Why? Because writing blog content can be time-intensive, laborious and come with little perceived benefit. But I can assure you that being active will breathe continued life into your website and give your donors the confidence that their support is being used well. Share good news. Promote your campaigns. Produce short pieces of content that give people a peek behind the scenes. If it helps, give others in your organisation the opportunity to contribute to the blog to share their view. This makes the job of maintaining the blog easier whilst at the same time provides a richer reading experience for visitors. Don't neglect your blog, and it will work harder for you the more you cultivate it.

> **Insider tip: get into a positive routine!**
>
> Just like adopting a new diet or exercise routine, if you approach maintaining your website with a negative attitude; something you "have to do" each month, you'll get frustrated and let things slip. To make things easier, break your tasks down into tiny chunks and schedule them in each week at the same time. For example, you might state that you're going to write a short blog post every Thursday to share some news with your supporters. Do this, every week, and share on social media to help kickstart a positive habit.

Adopting a marketing mindset

This book has taught you how to build the case for a new website, deal with the many challenges of management, and has touched upon some important aspects for measuring your ROI. But these are all theories and nice ideas until put into practice. The real message here is to adopt an organisation-wide marketing *mindset*, which means constantly seeing the marketing value in your everyday activities. To really do this you need more than just a part-time comms person or the services of an external marketing agency. External suppliers are great, but they will never see things the way that you do; from the inside. This mindset should permeate your team and reflect how your organisation works at an operational level. If you neglect your website and don't bother to market it properly, it will become another item sitting on the proverbial shelf, gathering dust and costing you money simply to maintain.

By choosing to adopt a marketing mindset, you will instead be finding marketing opportunities in everyday life. The activities that you and your team carry out daily, the impact you make and the stories you have to tell are bursting to get out. With a slight mindset shift, you can tune into these opportunities and express them through your comms channels.

The theory is simple but the practice can be more challenging as a level of commitment is needed and the payoff won't be instant. Here are a few tips to adopt and practice a marketing mindset.

Create a content calendar

A content calendar is exactly what it sounds like, and it enables you to organise your activities and schedule them well in advance. There are plenty of things happening that you can tap into, whether it's the weekly #CharityTuesday hashtag on Twitter, the annual Giving Tuesday or one of the many important dates of your own; put them in a calendar and create content in the run-up to the events. Moreover, make a point of publishing content on your own website every week, if you can. Put this as a recurring event on your calendar to get into the groove.

Share everything with others

Always be thinking about what you can share openly on your blog, social channels and in your newsletter. Lower your guard and open up your organisation and personality to the world. We value transparency and brands are having to work harder to engage and become part of the conversation. Don't be afraid to push the boundaries (within reason!) and seek to share content that your competitors might shy away from. *Fortune favours the brave.*

Be authentic

Take the time to understand *why* people follow and support you, and then speak genuinely to them. Don't worry too much about looking flash and scripted, just be yourself and your supporters will love you even more. That's not to say you shouldn't invest in more polished content, but ultimately you are speaking to people, so it's important that they see you as human too. Authenticity in marketing is becoming more and more important, as we shift toward a society that is ever more hostile toward ads and more open to relationships.

It really is all in the mindset, and the way to change the way you work to integrate consistent marketing activities into your organisation takes practice. By constantly seeking visibility in your everyday work, you'll build up your profile and enhance your impact massively over time.

Insider tip: be your own marketer!

As a digital provider to small charities, I find it an absolute blessing when somebody on the customer's team has a knowledge and passion for marketing. It just makes everything easier and more effective because they know what it takes to gain visibility. As an organisation you *could* outsource your thinking to a marketing agency, and there are certainly good reasons to do so, but know that there is *so much* you can already do in-house, right now, that can bring real value to your organisation. So be your own marketer!

Chapter 17:
PUTTING THIS INTO PRACTICE

We have covered an awful lot in this book. Who knew that so much went into planning, launching and marketing the humble old website! I hope you feel enlightened and inspired, and have obtained some genuinely useful information that you can begin putting into practice.

However, I am aware that information overload can be a real threat to progress, and if you feel overwhelmed I'd like to reassure you of a few things:

- You don't need to dwell on every topic outlined in this book
- Moving forward slowly is better than moving too quickly (or not moving at all)
- Your good intentions are half the battle.

In my professional life, on the projects I have worked on and led, as well as on the many side projects in my personal life, I have often found myself overwhelmed. When I feel overwhelmed I tend to have two responses: 1) bury my head in the sand and ignore everything I have to do, or 2) try to move forward too quickly without giving the task in hand enough thought. Both pacify me for a short period, but ultimately they delay the inevitable and lead to a less than desirable situation.

I have mapped out entire customer journeys without speaking to a single one of them. I have obsessed about the colour of a piece of text, despite nobody ever actually having read it. I have launched projects without having a business plan. I've spent thousands on boosted Facebook posts to promote websites that have gone nowhere.

My history is littered with failed projects, wasted money and spoiled opportunities.

Why am I telling you this? Because it is important to recognise that *everything* is a work in progress. Your project, your organisation, you. Without wishing to enter the territory of "self-help" too deeply I feel it is vital to point out that we must embrace the prospect of failure because, simply put; we cannot avoid it. And if we do somehow avoid failure, it only means we haven't strayed far enough beyond the confines of our comfort zone to experience it. When we embrace failure we become open to *learning*. It's difficult to really know what mistakes look like until you make then, and once you have made a few, you look back with a newfound strength and resilience in your area of focus.

I've learned a lot about digital technology (enough to write a book!) simply by *doing*, and you can too. So my advice to you moving forward is this:

- Take a couple of ideas from this book and experiment with them
- Don't go all in; but do enough to have a measurable outcome
- Try your best.

Whether you're embarking on a new website project, tuning up your current one or planning out a marketing campaign, the tools and advice given here should help you to understand and execute on your ideas more effectively. Don't be afraid to make mistakes along the way, but be sure to learn from them and integrate your learnings into future projects. As the classic book *Feel the Fear... and Do it Anyway* states: the only way to get rid of the fear of doing something is to go out and do it! Appreciating that there really is no "wrong way", and that even the most disastrous outcomes still hold some value, puts our minds at ease and liberates us from that consuming fear of putting a foot wrong. One step in front of the other, we move forward.

MY STORY

I meet a lot of people in business and when they hear my pitch I often get asked why I work with third sector organisations. The (somewhat correct) perception is that there is no money to be made working with charities, and everybody is in business to make money, so why on earth am I doing what I do?

The truth is, for me the idea of working only for money never made much sense. We spend so much of our lives doing a job, and it always seemed to me that if you "live for the weekend" your life seems shockingly short. It is more important, to me, to gain satisfaction during those weekdays than to save up my "living" for the weekend.

But more than this, I feel an urgency to have a positive impact in the world. In my younger, carefree days as a university graduate, my skills in website design were in high demand. I'd always enjoyed the free, artistic appeal of design, but soon enough the commercial industry was commoditising my skills and paying me a relatively decent rate for doing so. I worked on all kinds of projects with companies of varying sizes, but as I grew I realised that what I was doing was, at best, inconsequential. Sure, I might enhance shareholder value for my clients; but is that really how I want to look back on my working life?

In 2015 I started attending a quarterly charity event called *Soup*. If you're not familiar with such events, the idea essentially goes like this: several local charities pitch to a room of people to win a pot of money as contributed to by the audience. After the pitches have been heard, the audience votes for their preferred charity, and the winner receives the money to spend on the cause they outlined during their pitch. Whilst voting is occurring, attendees are each served a bowl of hot soup and a roll. This model, founded in the US city of Detroit, has been replicated in various cities across the world including Leeds, where I live.

Some of these pitches literally changed the course of my professional career.

One story in particular stands out in my mind. A woman who worked for a local homeless charity outlined the factors and conditions that contribute to entrenched rough sleeping. She spoke of a woman who, having been abused repeatedly by an immediate family member, a foster carer *and* later by her partner, had subsequently become homeless, vulnerable and incredibly untrusting of others as a result of her trauma. The very idea of "home" was tainted, and so the street seemed a viable option. The charity worker spent several weeks walking past the woman, smiling at her and making eye contact before eventually making an approach. Many rough sleepers are unconvinced by "the system", having had a poor previous experience, and so any organisation wishing to help must do so delicately. This was eye-opening, and moving.

I learned (and felt) a lot during these events, and having only become politically-aware a few years previous I realised how it all linked together. Social justice, fairness, equality; these are the opposite of the greedy hedonism that business and society at large seems to teach us.

At this point I was self-employed and it took me a while to figure out how I was going to start having the impact I increasingly wanted. I knew that I wanted to use the technical skills I honed over the years and that my approach should attempt to fix some of the underlying issues rather than simply tackle the symptoms. This was a huge undertaking to get my head around, and many times felt quite hopeless. I don't recommend weeknight drinking but it offers a welcome distraction when going through times of existential crises!

Then I had another epiphany. What if I could help improve the way that charities use technology to make them more effective? What if I stopped talking abstractly about my services as to attract any type of company and instead focused my proposition squarely on non-profit organisations? From a business perspective, it is far more elegant to take a market segment and gear your entire offering around their needs, than to try and please everybody. And frankly, the thinner end of the third sector wedge could certainly do with the help.

This was the realisation I needed to align my values with a business model that could have genuine impact. The path seems blatantly obvious when I look back, but in the words of Steve Jobs "you can only join the dots after the fact". I now work with charities of all sizes, providing consultancy, creative services and training to help them make an impact. And it has proven to be the most fulfilling time of my professional career so far.

The part I play is small, but each time a customer says "thank you, that really helps" or "wow, I didn't know you could do that!" and every time an organisation raises money for a project that I worked on, I get a little buzz. To take an active role in the growth of so many non-profit organisations and see the impact they are having is quite a special vantage point. I'm very happy to have found a sense of purpose in my work, and look forward to seeing where it leads me in the future.

GLOSSARY OF KEY TERMS

In this section I explain the technologies, tools and concepts covered in this book in easy to understand terms. Knowledge is power, and by grasping some key techno-speak you'll be able to broach meaningful conversations and strike better deals with technology suppliers more confidently, and ultimately produce better, more effective work.

Term	Definition
Agile	A project management philosophy that values collaboration, productivity and flexibility over more traditional methods that may be considered bureaucratic.
API	Application Programming Interface - the method by which two pieces of disparate software can communicate with each other to share data or functionality.
Brand identity	This refers to the visuality of your organisation and is interchangeable with the term "visual identity". Generally, this covers your logo, colours, typography, imagery and photographic style, but can

	also cover language and tone of voice.
Content strategy	The plan by which you develop and promote content such as blog articles, press releases and videos, that attracts supporters to your organisation.
Cookie	A file generated by a website and saved on your computer via the web browser. The file contains information about your visit, such as login details or text size preferences, and generally makes for a better, more customised visitor experience.
CRM	Customer Relationship Manager - enables you to intelligently manage and communicate with stakeholders, such as donors or volunteers. Send bulk emails, segment into people groups and trigger actions based on specified events.
Hashtag	On the web, tags are used to group related content together, and with the emergence of social media tags are preceded by the hash (#) character, hence the term "hashtag". You would use hashtags to take part in specific conversations, such as the popular

	#CharityTuesday tag on Twitter.
Internet of Things	This refers to a vision of the near-future where most household and personal electronic devices are fitted with sensors that collect and process data. Data is shared between devices to enable devices to work together efficiently.
Keyword	A word or phrase that best describes your product or service offering, most often used in the context of SEO.
KPI	Key Performance Indicator - KPIs are milestones which can indicate the success of a marketing campaign. In practice, they point to how close you might be to achieving your goal.
MVP	Minimum Viable Product - this refers to the most basic version of something (usually a piece of software) that serves its core purpose, providing a foundation upon which additional features can be added.
Persona	A fictional person that you create from user research in order to help you

	develop an experience that motivates or satisfies them in some way.
ROI	Return on Investment - a common term in business used to estimate the outcome of an expenditure to assess profitability.
SaaS	Software as a Service - a web or mobile application that exists to solve a specific problem, often in place of what may have traditionally been a service (i.e. software in place of a bookkeeper).
SEO	Search Engine Optimisation - the method by which a website can be ranked highly in search engines like Google.
Sitemap	A diagram that outlines the key pages on a website and describes the flow of information in a hierarchical fashion.
SSL	Secure Sockets Layer - a security certification for your website denoted by the small padlock icon seen in most internet browsers. An SSL certificate ensures that form data is encrypted when submitted.

Stakeholder	Any individual or representative group who have a vested interest in your organisation, such as trustees, donors and staff.
Theory of change	A common methodology used by social-purpose organisations to predict and plan impact. Typically, an end-goal is defined and the theory of change model is used to map the journey backwards from there.
UX design	User experience design - this refers to the process of researching and designing a product or service to directly address the needs of its specific users. Wireframes and user journeys are mapped out to define key objectives.
Web host/web server	The physical machine which stores your website. Think of it as a standard computer, but much more powerful and linked up to a wider network so it can serve your website to visitors quickly.

Web traffic	Technically, this refers to the data sent and received by visitors to your website, but it is more commonly used to refer to actual website visitors. In context you might say "I want more web traffic" which in practice would mean that you want more visitors to your website.
Wireframe	A low-fidelity model, often simply a pen and paper sketch, of a web page to demonstrate the layout and flow of information.

USEFUL RESOURCES

Throughout this book I have referenced various tools and software that I use in my own work. I have collated these here, with a brief description of each, for your convenience.

Name	Description
Hotjar (hotjar.com)	Anonymously record your website visitors to spot patterns and uncover any usability problems. Also place interactive surveys and polls on your website to collect visitor feedback.
Leadfeeder (leadfeeder.com)	Identify which companies people who visit your website work for - useful if scouting for corporate sponsors.
Gloomaps (gloomaps.com)	Quickly create a sitemap for your website for free.

Anchor FM (anchor.fm)	Create a podcast for free. Record or upload your podcast content, and edit it to include intro/outro music.
Canva (canva.com)	Create social media graphics, infographics, posters, flyers and other creative materials.
Ahrefs (ahrefs.com/backlink-checker)	Find out how many websites link to yours.
WebAIM (webaim.org)	Web Accessibility in Mind, a resource providing guidance for organisations to make web content accessible to those with disabilities
WAVE (wave.webaim.org)	Test your website for basic accessibility issues and get help on how to fix any problems

WordPress (wordpress.com) Drupal (drupal.org) Joomla (joomla.org)	Open-source Content Management Systems (CMS) enabling you to control the content on your website.
WooCommerce (woocommerce.com)	A popular e-commerce plugin for WordPress that enables you to sell physical and digital products through your website.

ACKNOWLEDGEMENTS

Writing this book has been a hugely rewarding experience for me, and I'm immensely proud of what has been achieved. However, this would not have been possible without the support of a number of people, and I would like to use this space to thank them for their contributions.

First and foremost I'd like to thank Liz, my partner, who has not only given me a lot of practical input on the content and structure of the book, but who is also a source of so much wonderful encouragement and optimism in my life. She has a way of making me feel like anything is possible. Thank you, Liz, for everything you do.

I would also like to thank Will, my brother, who not only illustrated the cover of this book, has been a rock throughout my personal and professional life. Will, you are always there when I need you. I can count on you for a sympathetic ear, a confidant in business and an authoritative voice on graphic design. Thank you.

My thanks, also, to the people who were good enough to let me interview them for this book. Carley, Mandy, Vikram and Emmelie - hearing your stories was a privilege and really helped to spur my ambition for sharing them with others.

Finally I would like to extend my thanks to Howard Lake of UK Fundraising for writing an excellent foreword, Ian

Hurlock and the team at Lightful for their ongoing support, Keith Abbott of Michael Terence Publishing for guiding me through the publication process, and Daniel Priestley, author of Key Person of Influence, the book that convinced me to write my own in the first place.

*Available worldwide from Amazon
and all good bookstores*

_____

www.mtp.agency

www.facebook.com/mtp.agency

@mtp_agency

www.ingramcontent.com/pod-product-compliance
Lightning Source LLC
LaVergne TN
LVHW022314060326
832902LV00020B/3459